STUDY GUIDE

OPERATING IN KINGDOM AUTHORITY

STUDY GUIDE

OPERATING IN KINGDOM AUTHORITY

BY Dr. Kevin L. Zadai

Please note that Warrior Notes publishing style capitalizes certain pronouns in Scripture that refer to the Father, Son, and Holy Spirit, which may differ from some publishers' styles. Take note that the name "satan" and related names are not capitalized. We choose not to acknowledge him, even to the point of violating accepted grammatical rules. All emphasis within Scripture quotations is the author's own.

Cover design: Virtually Possible Designs

For more information about our school, go to www.warriornotesschool.com.
Reach us on the internet: www.Kevinzadai.com
ISBN 13 TP: 978-1-6631-0029-0

Warrior Notes Publishing
P O Box 1288
Destrehan, LA 70047

For more information about our school, go to www.warriornotesschool.com. Reach us on the internet: www.Kevinzadai.com

Dedication

I dedicate this book to the Lord Jesus Christ. When I died during surgery and met with Jesus on the other side, He insisted that I return to life on the earth and that I help people with their destinies. Because of Jesus' love and concern for people, the Lord has actually chosen to send a person back from death to help everyone who will receive that help so that his or her destiny and purpose is secure in Him. I want You, Lord, to know that when You come to take me to be with You someday, it is my sincere hope that people remember not me, but the revelation of Jesus Christ that You have revealed through me. I want others to know that I am merely being obedient to Your Heavenly calling and mission, which is to reveal Your plan for the fulfillment of the divine destiny for each of God's children.

Acknowledgments

In addition to sharing my story with everyone through the book *Heavenly Visitation: A Guide to the Supernatural,* God has commissioned me to write over fifty books and study guides. Most recently, the Lord gave me the commission to produce this study guide, *Operating in Kingdom Authority.* This study guide addresses some of the revelations concerning the areas that Jesus reviewed and revealed to me through the Word of God and by the Spirit of God during several visitations. I want to thank everyone who has encouraged me, assisted me, and prayed for me during the writing of this work. Special thanks to my wonderful wife, Kathi, for her love and dedication to the Lord and me. Thank you to a great staff for the wonderful job editing this book. Special thanks as well to all my friends who know about *Operating in Kingdom Authority* and how to operate in this for the next move of God's Spirit!

Contents

Introduction

As a called and chosen one, you must submit yourself to the mentoring of the Holy Spirit and to discipleship. Proverbs 9:10 tells us that the fear of the Lord is the beginning of wisdom; however, it is also the beginning of understanding authority because if you fear God and are broken, humble, and submitted to the Lord, you will repent and stay under the mighty hand of God. When you humble yourself under the mighty hand of God, He will promote you and lift you up in due season (1 Peter 5:6). You will do very well in life and fulfill your call by understanding this.

We need to get back into the simplicity of understanding God's kingdom. God's Spirit is advancing; His Kingdom is within you and advancing through you! Allow the Holy Spirit to manifest through you. We are to build one another up to reach maturity and be in the unity of the faith (Ephesians 4:13). Go from one who has been *called* to one who has been *chosen*; learn to operate in kingdom authority and get ready for what you have been chosen to do!

CHAPTER 1

Qualified and Accountable

"For many are called, but few are chosen."
—Matthew 22:14

DISCUSSION:
You need to acquire leadership principles as a student, a disciple, and a leader. You must begin to think of yourself as a leader and walk in leadership because so much needs to be done in the kingdom. God, Himself is calling many people, but few are chosen. Everyone is called, but many people are not chosen because they do not qualify. You must partake in a discipleship program and be mentored by the Holy Spirit. The gifts of the Spirit are good for operating and building up the body of Christ (1 Corinthians 12:4-11).

EQUIPPED FOR THE WORK OF MINISTRY

- **EPHESIANS 4:11-13:**
  And He Himself gave some to be apostles, some prophets, some evangelists, and some pastors and teachers, for the equipping of the saints for the work of ministry, for the edifying of the body of Christ, till we all come to the unity of

the faith and of the knowledge of the Son of God, to a perfect man, to the measure of the stature of the fullness of Christ;

- The Fivefold Ministry gifts are to build up the body to maturity, be in the unity of the faith, and then go out and minister (Ephesians 4:11-13, 1 Corinthians 12:28-31).
- Ministry gifts prepare you for what you are chosen to do, not just called.
- Many people never get chosen, even though they are called. You must be brought up to the place where you qualify and are accountable.

What is the purpose of the Fivefold Ministry?

____

____

____

____

UNDERSTANDING AUTHORITY

❖ **COLOSSIANS 2:15 NLT:**

In this way, he disarmed the spiritual rulers and authorities. He shamed them publicly by his victory over them on the cross.

- Our enemy satan does not want people to understand authority or dominion.

- If a Christian understood authority and took authority, satan would start losing his kingdom piece by piece, and it would diminish in a greater manner.
- Jesus already destroyed the works of the devil on the cross and made a show of satan openly triumphing over him, but it must be enforced.

❖ **HOSEA 4:6:**

My people are destroyed for lack of knowledge. Because you have rejected knowledge, I also will reject you from being priest for Me; Because you have forgotten the law of your God, I also will forget your children.

- People perish because they lack understanding. They do not have a vision, and they do not understand.
- People do not have the manifestation of authority and dominion because they do not implement it.
- The devil does not want you to understand that the authority you have been given is through Jesus Christ.
- God is a king and sits on a throne, and He has authority from that throne; everything must bow, and everything must submit to Him.
- God rules over His domain, and it is called dominion.
- We need to enforce our authority using the name of Jesus and the blood and power words like these.

- We need to use these power words because that is what destroys and enforces the destruction of the enemy.
- Power words are amazing and powerful doctrinal truths given by the Lord. That is why we teach about repentance, humility, brokenness, the blood of Jesus, the name of Jesus, and many others.
- The power words destroy and enforce the destruction of the enemy.
- The revelation of kingdom authority comes through the ministry gifts.

Are you exercising your authority by using the power words?

____

____

____

____

KINGDOM, AUTHORITY, AND RANK

❖ **DANIEL 10:13:**

But the prince of the kingdom of Persia withstood me twenty-one days; and behold, Michael, one of the chief princes, came to help me, for I had been left alone there with the kings of Persia.

- Angels also have authority, and Heaven is set up like the military because everything is by rank.

- Like Michael, there are mighty angels, and archangels are very authoritative and powerful.
- Warrior angels are also powerful and authoritative. Then there are messenger angels, recording angels, and different special forces of angels.
- Some angels don't have wings, and they look like people. You have a kingdom, and you have authority, and you have rank.
- The body of Christ has the highest rank of all.
- A human being is saved, baptized in the Holy Spirit, sanctified, and set apart for God's glory.
- You are the most powerful individual in existence on this earth.
- The Holy Spirit does that in your life by the blood and the name of Jesus.

What are some of the ranks of the angels?

____

____

____

____

GOD'S SPIRIT IS ADVANCING

- **ZECHARIAH 4:6 NLT:**

  Then he said to me, "This is what the LORD says to Zerubbabel: It is not by force nor by strength, but by my Spirit, says the LORD of Heaven's Armies.

- The people were not drunk, but this fulfilled what the Prophet Joel had prophesied.
- The Spirit of God advanced through Jesus, starting through the prophets and Moses.
- David was anointed, and all the prophets were anointed.
- The Spirit of God was in Jesus and upon Jesus.
- The disciples became apostles because they had the anointing upon them.
- The disciples were baptized in the Holy Spirit and filled with the Holy Spirit.
- The first sign of the New Testament church was the Day of Pentecost because that is when the Holy Spirit came and filled us up.
- Jesus came and walked the earth and showed us how to walk in power.

What happens when you are baptized and filled with the Holy Spirit?

____

____

____

____

THE KINGDOM IS WITHIN YOU

❖ **EPHESIANS 4:8:**

Therefore He says: "When He ascended on high, He led captivity captive, And gave gifts to men."

- When Jesus descended into the belly of the earth, it says He took captivity captive, and then He ascended on high. He distributed gifts that were given to men.
- The distribution of the Holy Spirit and all the gifting is for all of us to have gifts inside of us.
- Everyone needs to do their part and be encouraged that the Holy Spirit wants to preach the Word of God and demonstrate the Word of God through each one of us.
- The kingdom of God is actually within you, not just upon you.
- The kingdom of God in us is advancing, and the revelation of the Holy Spirit is so important.
- In Heaven, I saw how even the angels were involved with us.
- I saw the saints cheering us on, people who had done their part, who left us and went on to be with the Lord.

- They are all very well briefed in Heaven and are cheering us on because they know what is ahead for us.
- They know we have a big part to play in this end-time scenario.
- The key here is understanding our authority, and that authority is Jesus Christ seated on His throne and honored.
- Jesus, the name above all names that everything must bow and submit to Him.

Do you know what gifts have been given to you?

____

____

____

____

TEACH WITH AUTHORITY

❖ **MATTHEW 7:28-29:**

And so it was, when Jesus had ended these sayings, that the people were astonished at His teaching, for He taught them as one having authority, and not as the scribes.

- The name of Jesus is the most powerful word we can speak on this earth. When Jesus taught on the earth, the people were astonished at His teaching.

- At that time, there were many rabbis, Pharisees, Sadducees, and well-known teachers in the synagogues, teaching all the rituals and laws to many disciples.
- However, it says, Jesus taught them as one having authority and not as the scribes, who were the Pharisees.
- When I was in Bible college, I noticed they presented all these different opinions and views of what people believe could be in the Bible.
- Then they said what they officially believed but that others believed differently, but I want to teach as one having authority.
- We need to teach as one who has authority, making it clear that two or three Scriptures support—the absolute truth of the Word of God.
- Always go to the teachings of Jesus because He taught in black and white with no grey areas to try to figure out. Jesus taught with authority.
- Jesus was a king that was preexistent from the foundation of the world, and was slain from the foundation of the world.
- Jesus has a throne in Heaven.

❖ **JOHN 17:21-24:**

That they all may be one, as You, Father, *are* in Me, and I in You; that they also may be one in Us, that the world may believe that You sent Me. And the glory which You gave Me I have given them, that they may be one just as We are one: I in them, and You in Me; that they may be made perfect in one, and that the world may know that You have sent Me, and have loved them as You have loved Me. "Father, I desire that they also whom You gave Me may

be with Me where I am, that they may behold My glory which You have given Me; for You loved Me before the foundation of the world.

- Remember that Jesus was preexistent and a king.
- The foundation of the world was made by Him.
- Everything that exists, including you, was thought of long before you were made.
- On earth, Jesus walked among men, but He was God.
- The Pharisees and the scribes noticed that Jesus was speaking with authority.

❖ When the anointing of the Holy Spirit is teaching, and the Holy Spirit anoints someone, it will have authority because the Holy Spirit is God. He is going to speak with authority. You can tell if a minister is yielding to the Spirit of God because it will be noticeable.

- The disciples, when they became apostles, people noted that they had been with Jesus (Acts 4:13).
- The disciples turned the world upside down.
- People need to be trained and fully convinced to speak with authority.

Are you fully convinced that you can speak with authority?

____

____

____

____

BENEFITS OF AUTHORITY

DISCUSSION:

As a believer, you need to understand everything that has to do with life and godliness because God has given you everything you need. Second Peter says that we are partakers of the divine nature; we have been given all these precious promises, and then we need to know what our benefits are and what those entail. The goal of every Christian should be to be fully convinced of what they believe in and why they believe it. They need to know that Jesus Christ is full of authority, and He is fully convinced that you will succeed. Jesus does not ever think that you will fail, nor do the angels. When you encounter evil spirits, they know when you know and understand your authority and when you don't know.

- **2 PETER 1:3-4:**

  As His divine power has given to us all things that *pertain* to life and godliness, through the knowledge of Him who called us by glory and virtue, by which have been given to us exceedingly great and precious promises, that through these you may be partakers of the divine nature, having escaped the corruption *that is* in the world through lust.

- When you teach, you speak with authority.
- You have this attitude, and people notice that you have authority.
- You are sure and fully convinced of your authority.

❖ Even animals like horses can sense if you are unsure of yourself, and they will take advantage of that and take you for a ride, which is exactly what happens with devils. In the Book of Acts 19:13-17, the devils knew the seven sons of Sceva did not know who they were and were not known in hell, so the devils took advantage of them.

- You cannot just be like a parrot repeating something you have heard.
- When you pray for people, you must have authority.
- You have authority because you are fully convinced, and God tells you to pray.
- God tells us to believe, and He tells us to drive out devils.
- God tells us to heal the sick and raise the dead.
- God tells us to preach Jubilee debt cancellation.
- God tells us to preach the good news of the gospel.
- God tells us to tell people they are delivered and free.
- God, who is rich in mercy, did all this work, this mighty salvation, and gave us this authority because He loves people (Ephesians 2:4-10).
- People's hearts need to be enlightened.

- When you walk in authority, you must teach it, not just do it yourself; you must implement it.
- You have to make it, so people understand how to walk in authority.

Do people notice that you have an attitude of walking in authority? If not, how can you make a change in this area?

____

____

____

____

REALITY OF A NEW CREATION

❖ **2 CORINTHIANS 5:17:**

Therefore, if anyone *is* in Christ, *he* is a new creation; old things have passed away; behold, all things have become new.

- Nothing changes with you and your soul that day when you get saved.
- You are now born again in your spirit, and the old passes away—you are a new creation. It is spiritual, but your mind, will, and emotions are part of the soul.
- You must implement this into people's souls to cause them to be renewed in their minds by the Word of God.

❖ **ROMANS 12:2-3:**

And do not be conformed to this world, but be transformed by the renewing of your mind, that you may prove what *is* that good and acceptable and perfect will of God.

- It is often a battle to renew your mind.
- Walking in authority on the earth includes teaching in authority so that people understand the soul realm and not just the spirit realm.
- You must expose yourself to the Word of God, the Spirit of God, the workings of the manifestations of God, and the encounters that the Spirit wants to give all of us to where it becomes our reality. It becomes experiential.
- You must have experiential knowledge and a relationship with Jesus, the Word who became flesh.
- The people noticed that Jesus was different, and that is where the body of Christ has to be today.
- The world needs to see Christians are different in a good way.
- Christians must be known by their authority and that God is with them and they have favor.

How can you walk in authority and the favor of God?

____

____

____

____

AUTHORITY OVER DISEASE

- ❖ **MATTHEW 8:1-3:**

When Jesus came down from the mountainside, large crowds followed him. A man with leprosy came and knelt before him and said, "Lord, if you are willing, you can make me clean." Jesus reached out his hand and touched the man. "I am willing," he said. "Be clean!" Immediately he was cleansed of his leprosy.

- There were times when Jesus went from one place to another, and when He came down from the mountainside, people followed Him.
- Jesus did not invite them, but the people would just gather if Jesus was in town preaching and miracles were happening.
- There are different levels of faith, and how people receive their healing.
- Jesus purposefully touched the leper because it showed that he had authority over disease even though it was highly contagious.

- ❖ **MATTHEW 8:5-10:**

When Jesus had entered Capernaum, a centurion came to him, asking for help. "Lord" he said, "my servant lies at home paralyzed, suffering terribly." Jesus said to him, "Shall I come and heal him?" The centurion replied, "Lord, I do not deserve to have you come under my roof. But just say the word, and my servant will be healed. For I myself am a man under authority, with soldiers under me. I tell this one, 'Go' and he goes; and that one, 'Come,' and he

comes. I say to my servant, 'Do this,' and he does it." When Jesus heard this, he was amazed and said to those following him, "Truly I tell you, I have not found anyone in Israel with such great faith."

- Great faith is understanding authority.
- Great faith is all about submission.
- Great faith is all about humility.
- You don't question authority.
- You do what you are told to do.

DISCUSSION:

Jesus equates the centurion's understanding of authority to great faith, which is never taught. The whole main point of this passage is that great faith is understanding authority. The centurion was a man under authority, having soldiers under him. He says to one, go, and he goes, and to another come, and he comes. The centurion understood that this is how it was with the military because, in the military, you do what you are told. The centurion just gives out a command, and it is done. He was under the authority of Caesar and Pilot. He gave out orders, but he also took orders. When Jesus heard this, He marveled.

How have you received healing?

____

____

____

____

CHAPTER 2

The Holy Spirit and Power

And you know that God anointed Jesus of Nazareth with the Holy Spirit and with power. Then Jesus went around doing good and healing all who were oppressed by the devil, for God was with him.
—Acts 10:38 NLT

DISCUSSION:

Throughout the Bible, we can see that Jesus healed in several ways, all by revelation on authority. His ministry was done by the power of the Holy Spirit, not as a Son of God, but by a Son of man anointed by the power of the Holy Spirit. As such, we are to do the same things today, and then we will do greater things.

- ❖ **<u>JOHN 14:12:</u>**

  Most assuredly, I say to you, he who believes in Me, the works that I do he will do also; and greater works than these he will do, because I go to my Father.

- Jesus healed without any conversation.
- When walking in authority, you do not have to say anything, and people get healed, delivered, and even raised from the dead.
- Jesus cast out the spirits with a word—not a conversation.
- There are many modes of walking in authority.
- Jesus was a fulfillment of what was spoken about Him by Isaiah the prophet.
- Jesus Himself bore our infirmities and bore our sicknesses.
- Jesus was healing, but he hadn't died yet. God was healing, delivering, and ministering to people on credit because it hadn't happened physically. It was a fulfillment of what Isaiah said.

What are some of the ways Jesus healed people?

____

____

____

____

WALKING IN THE KINGDOM

❖ **<u>LUKE 9:58:</u>**

And Jesus said to him, "Foxes have holes and birds of the air *have* nests, but the Son of Man has nowhere to lay *His* head."

- There was a conversation between them, and Jesus said He did not even have a place to rest.
- Then another of His disciples said, "Let me first bury my father." Jesus hinted that He wasn't staying very long anyway on the earth.
- Jesus said, "Follow Me, and let the dead bury their dead" (Matthew 8:22).
- You chose to follow Jesus.
- You are separated now.
- You must let go of things, family, and friends and follow Jesus.

❖ There is a certain point where people do not want to go on with you and with your faith. The Lord is asking you to go out and minister, then things will start to pull on you and pull you back in.

- Understanding authority is understanding that your life is not your own.
- You will have tests to obey and follow the Lord.
- When you are under authority, you are under command.
- I have had these tests where the Lord told me, "I would not do that. You are going to do what I told you to do."
- I have had the Lord tell me, "You are not answering that call because it will take away what I have already told you to do."
- When you are under authority, you are under command.

Has the Lord told you things He wanted you to do?

____

____

____

____

LITTLE FAITH

❖ **MATTHEW 8:23-26:**

Now when He got into a boat, His disciples followed Him. And suddenly, a great tempest arose on the sea so that the boat was covered with the waves. But He was asleep. Then His disciples came to *Him* and awoke Him, saying, "Lord, save us! We are perishing!" But He said to them, "Why are you fearful, O you of little faith?"

- Jesus' disciples followed Him and got into the boat. As they crossed, the waves started to cover the boat, but Jesus was asleep because the Father had already told Him to go to the other side.
- The disciples came to Jesus and said, "We are perishing. Don't you care?"
- Jesus said, "Why are you so fearful?" Jesus taught them through all the ways He walked with them and healed them.
- The centurion said to speak the word, and it will be done.
- When you are fearful, you have little faith.

- You are hard of hearing and do not understand authority.
- Jesus said to the wind to shut up, and the waves immediately obeyed Him.

DISCUSSION:

After they came to the other side, two demon-possessed men went out of the tombs, and they were fearsome, and no one could pass by. They were crying out and saying what do you have to do with us, Jesus, Son of God? Have you come to torment before time (Romans 8:28-29)? The demons understood who Jesus is in eternity, the Son of God. Jesus told them to shut up because He did not want them to announce Him as being the Son of God. He wanted to be known and walked as the Son of man for our benefit.

Has the Lord revealed that you were operating in fear and not faith?

____

____

____

____

TERRITORIAL AUTHORITY

❖ **MATTHEW 8:30-31:**

Now a good way off from them there was a herd of many swine feeding. So the demons begged Him, saying, "If You cast us out, permit us to go away into the herd of swine."

- Jesus did not dispute the demons.
- Jesus did not send the demons out of the area but into swine.
- Jesus did not send them to torment; He cast them out.
- The demons want to stay in the same area they were in.
- Demons have developed their own territorial authority and influence.
- The demons are assigned areas.

Why did Jesus allow the demons to go into the swine?

____

____

____

____

THE COMMISSION GRANTS AUTHORITY

DISCUSSION:

Jesus walked in this authority, and He gave us so many clues about how to do this so we can walk in this kingdom's authority. Jesus' Word is very powerful, His touch is very powerful, and His presence is very powerful. One way of healing was Jesus would just touch. Another way of healing was that He had the centurion's faith and spoke the Word. Jesus rebuked the winds and the waves just like He would a demon, and they listened as though they were people. The kingdom was working and advancing because Jesus was continually healing people and casting out devils.

- **MATTHEW 28:18:**

And Jesus came and spoke to them, saying, "All authority has been given to Me in heaven and on earth."

- Jesus walked in authority.
- Jesus gives us all authority.
- Meditate on the Word of God
- Realize that you have authority regardless of physical size and do not need to be boisterous.
- Sometimes Jesus didn't say a word, sometimes He said a word, and sometimes He just touched.
- The demons and the wind could be rebuked.
- Sometimes Jesus showed up, and the demons started to manifest, and we will experience this too.
- As a believer who has been given authority, size, gender, or ethnic background does not matter to walk in authority.
- It includes everyone.

What is a specific situation where you used your authority? What was the outcome?

____

____

____

____

WOMEN IN MINISTRY

❖ **MATTHEW 10:1:**

And when He had called His twelve disciples to *Him,* He gave them power over unclean spirits, to cast them out, and heal all kinds of sickness and all kinds of disease.

- Interestingly, a woman has the ability as a believer to cast out devils, but they cannot minister in some churches because they are a woman.
- According to Scripture, women are commanded to preach the gospel. Women are commanded to cast out devils, heal the sick, and raise the dead. You must be careful when rules are made regarding certain things you cannot do in the church.
- We must allow the Holy Spirit to dictate what we believe in the Word of God. Authority has to do with a name and a kingdom, and it was given to everyone.
- Everyone has been bought with a price, and Jesus died for everyone.
- Everyone can have salvation, and it is up to us.
- Everyone born again and Spirit-filled believes in the Word of God.
- Believers have the power to drive out devils because they have the name of Jesus, and they are born again.
- No excuse exists because every believer can walk in full authority as Jesus did.
- The kingdom is advancing at an alarming rate, and it is mighty.
- God gave us all the Holy Spirit who believed in it.

As a believer, what do we have the authority to do?

____

____

____

____

ALL THINGS ARE POSSIBLE

❖ **<u>MARK 9:23:</u>**

Jesus said to him, “If you can believe all things are possible to him who believes.”

- A profound statement is made when Jesus said if you can believe, all things are possible to him who believes.
- There needs to be more emphasis on this in believers today.
- Jesus said you could come into a place where if there is a mountain in your way, you can send it away; it can be removed (Mark 11:23). You do this with your words.
- You believe in your heart, not in your head.
- Say with your mouth, and it will be done.

How are you to believe?

____

____

____

____

SURE THINGS

❖ **MATTHEW 7:7-8:**

Ask, and it will be given to you; seek and you will find; knock, and it will be opened to you. For everyone who asks receives; the one who seeks finds, and to the one who knocks, the door will be opened.

- Prayer takes on a new level when you think about asking, receiving, knocking, seeking, finding, and opening the door.
- These are sure things—they are signed, sealed, and delivered. If you ask, you are going to receive. In the original language, the word *ask* is the word *demand*.
- When you know God's will, you do not just ask but demand.
- You have authority, so you take authority.
- You enforce God's will by not requesting but by commanding.
- When God tells you something, you choose to obey it.
- If you love God, you will obey Him.

How are we to pray?

____

____

____

____

BALANCE OF THE GOSPEL

❖ **ROMANS 8:8:**

So then, those who are in the flesh cannot please God.

- There are a lot of weak Christians who just talk about God's love and forgiveness, and it is just an emotional thing, not the true gospel.
- When adversity comes, they cannot make the step to be a kingdom person walking in authority.
- Do not give provision to the flesh
- If you yield to the flesh, you cannot please God. You are an enemy of God if you yield to the flesh. Yielding to the flesh works against the Spirit.

DISCUSSION:

Immature Christians will talk about the love of God, saying He accepts you as you are, He loves you, and they only bask in His love and presence. When you teach them about repentance, forgiveness, the blood of Jesus, humility, brokenness, that we suffer for doing what is good, and if you love me, you are going to obey me, which is the balance of the gospel, they do not want to grow up. They do not know how to walk in authority to where they speak to the mountains, and they are removed, and He commands us to believe and not doubt. They sit and bask in a false sense that God loves me just like I am. Well, He might not. He might think, *You are not the way I want you to be.*

❖ **JOHN 14:15:**

If you love Me, keep My commandments.

- You may need to take a couple of steps and walk in holiness.
- When you walk in righteousness, you are no longer a child.
- Immature Christians cannot be addressed as spiritual.
- You are carnal on milk and should be on meat (1 Corinthians 3:1-2).
- You need to take the next step and become mature and spiritual.
- You need to please God by obeying His commands.
- Believe that nothing will be impossible and return to the centurion type of faith, which understands authority.
- Jesus was full of the authority of God, He was anointed of God, and He went around doing good and healing everyone oppressed by the devil (Acts 10:38).
- That is God's plan for you and is what we will do.

CHAPTER 3

The Kingdom Manifested

By faith we understand that the universe was created by the word of God, so that what is seen was not made out of things that are visible.
—Hebrews 11:3 ESV

DISCUSSION:

We need to walk in great authority so that every devil knows that we are walking in authority, and they back off. When Jesus tells us, we speak the Word, and it will be done. Jesus did not have to go someplace to have people healed or delivered. Peter's shadow healed as he walked by people. Paul was able to be at a church service in the Spirit because the power of God was present, and there was a manifestation of something. Paul did not have to be there physically to do what he was called to do.

- **2 CORINTHIANS 5:20a:**

  Now then, we are ambassadors for Christ, as though God were pleading through us:

- We are ambassadors, and we are sent.
- When you are sent, whatever happens, you know you were sent.
- If you are sent, and you are under authority.
- You do not choose to go when you are sent and hope it works out fine.
- We need only to do what the Father tells us to do.

DISCUSSION:

The disciples were supposed to do the speaking to the winds and the waves. Jesus believed that the disciples would get it based on how they had seen Jesus implement authority in many ways against the devils and sickness. Jesus was disappointed that they were not taking care of it. They should have understood that if He said they were going to the other side and the Father sent them, no one would get hurt. They obeyed because they had authority over the devil to speak to the winds and the waves.

❖ **<u>MATTHEW 8:26-27:</u>**

But He said to them, "Why are you fearful, O you of little faith?" Then He arose and rebuked the winds and the sea, and there was a great calm. So the men marveled, saying, "Who can this be, that even the winds and the sea obey him?"

- You need to take accountability and responsibility.
- Weak Christians do not understand the love of God.
- God's love is expressed by obedience—that is how we tell God we love Him.

- Obedience has to do with being under authority and being submissive.

❖ If you ask permission to speak to your Commanding Officer in the Armed Forces, you better be careful and ensure that what you are about to ask is not questioning that person's authority. It will be taken that way unless it is a valid question.

- If you do not act immediately, you are questioning authority and not under authority. You think that you know more.
- If God tells you to do something, you must obey Him.
- Many say, "I feel like I'm out of God's will and can't feel God."
- I have found over the years that they feel that way because God wanted them to go in a certain direction, and they did not do it.

❖ There is a solution when you are in the desert, out of place, or have departed from the path because of an act of disobedience.

- I tell people to go back in their minds, in their hearts, and find out from the Holy Spirit where they got off, where they disobeyed, and revisit that and get it right and repent.
- If it is too late to do something He told you, then just repent, and the Holy Spirit will reroute you in a direction to get you back on track.

- Jesus sends us, and He tells us to do things.
- Christians with weak faith think God just loves them and excuses their sin.
- Jesus loves you, but He also disciplines you.
- You want to have great faith, understand authority, and submit to Jesus.

What should you do to get back on track when you have departed from God's path?

____

____

____

____

PLEASE GOD

❖ **1 JOHN 3:22:**

And whatever we ask we receive from Him, because we keep his commandments, and do those things that are pleasing in his sight.

- If Jesus says something to you, you do it and don't say a word; you go and do it—period.
- I have noticed many good people are opportunists. What this means is if an opportunity presents itself, they just take it.

- They do not consider that it might be the wrong path and could include even good opportunities that have to do with ministry.
- Jesus did not operate like this because many people did not get healed.
- They did not get healed because Jesus was not sent to them.

❖ **ACTS 3:6:**

Then Peter said, "Silver and gold I do not have, but what I do have I give you: In the name of Jesus Christ of Nazareth, rise up and walk."

- We read about this Scripture in the Book of Acts at the Gate Beautiful.
- Jesus walked by there all the time, but it was not until after He left and the Holy Spirit came upon the disciples, who became apostles, that they were sent, and the man was healed there.
- Many people were not ministered to during Jesus' three and a half years of ministry.
- The Lord may direct you not to pray for people because they are in disobedience.
- People are in a predicament because they have chosen to disobey the Lord, which is then working against them.
- Jesus is always willing to heal, help, protect and get people back on track.

Why were people not healed?

____

____

____

____

GREATER REWARD

❖ **HEBREWS 11:6:**

But without faith it is impossible to please *Him*, for he who comes to God must believe that He is, and *that* He is a rewarder of those who diligently seek Him.

- There must be repentance and obedience.
- Extreme grace equates everything with the love of God, but what about those who are obedient and always follow what the Holy Spirit is saying, who have made great sacrifices in their life?
- I know people who have obeyed, and it has cost them much. What about those people? They will have a greater reward.
- Enoch having faith, loved God, and he was not because he pleased God (Hebrews 11:5).
- Without faith it is impossible to please God.
- Great faith is understanding authority.

❖ To have the faith talked about in Hebrews, the Enoch type of faith, you must be known as someone who pleases God. Without faith, it is impossible to please God, and you must believe it exists.

- The devils believe that it exists, so it must be even greater than that.
- What reward is greater for those than just believing that God exists? It is the step of obedience.
- You diligently seek Him.
- He is a rewarder of those who diligently seek Him.
- When you seek God, you must be willing to obey Him.
- When you seek God, fast, and pray, the Lord gives you instructions.

❖ Sometimes the Lord will tell me to do something, which is not easy, and this is not being taught. Extreme grace teaches that God loves me, and He understands me. He made me this way, and then there is no accountability. You never actually get healed or delivered, and you are stuck.

- You cannot make people feel comfortable and have them camp there.
- People are broken and need healing and deliverance.
- People need to mature.
- You need to help people understand God's perfect will for them.
- We are ambassadors sent into the enemy's camp.
- We are taking from the enemy and looting what he has stolen.
- God is going to call you, but then He is going to choose you.

When you seek Him, are there times when you didn't obey?

____

____

____

____

CHOSEN BY GOD

❖ **MATTHEW 22:14:**

For many are called, but few are chosen.

- If you are called, you will walk in the authority of the head of the church, which means that every devil in hell knows who you are because they know who Jesus is.
- Jesus had the twelve, then He trained seventy and sent them out (Luke 10:1). When they came back, they were surprised that it worked. The demons listened to them.
- They watched Jesus do it, and He gave them authority to do it.
- They were babies and got caught up knowing it worked, but they should have known it would work. They were immature.
- When your name is written in the Lamb's Book of Life, demons listen to you because you are a son of God, and your name is written in Heaven. The demons know your name is written in Heaven.

- We do not need to sensationalize encounters and experiences people have with God.
- We are to expect people to have encounters and times of visitation.
- The body of Christ needs to mature.
- We are to be encountering the Holy Spirit strongly with signs and wonders (Mark 16:17-18).

❖ After a conference on my day off, while I am recording, I can do this by the power of the Holy Spirit. It is not something I would particularly choose to do at that time, but it is so powerful what the Spirit is doing to change people's thinking.

- It is profitable to help people.
- You should expect a sign and a wonder to happen.
- You should expect the power of God to come and help you in any situation—even on your day off.
- You should expect the Holy Spirit to resurrect you and do something that manifests the kingdom of Heaven on earth.

What are you expecting God to do for you?

____

____

____

____

THE SAME BAPTISMS

- ❖ **MATTHEW 20:22:**

But Jesus answered and said, "You do not know what you ask. Are you able to drink the cup that I am about to drink, and be baptized with the baptism that I am baptized with?" They said to Him, "We are able."

- Jesus said that they did not know what they asked.
- He said, "Can you drink the cup I am about to drink and be baptized with the same baptism I am baptized with?"
- They said to Him, "We are able." The wording here reflects that they did not know what they were saying and did not understand it.

- ❖ **MATTHEW 20:23:**

So He said to them, "You will indeed drink My cup, and be baptized with the baptism that I am baptized with; but to sit on My right hand and on My left is not Mine to give, but *it is for those* for whom it is prepared by My Father."

- Jesus had to submit to get the authority He has.
- You come to the communion table with the right heart and attitude. You sit at the table and discern the body of the Lord.
- Communion is a sacred time—taking the bread and cup, which represents Jesus' body.
- If you do not discern, you could drink judgment upon yourself.

- People are weak and sick and die early because they do not discern the Lord's body.
- The same baptism means you are separate and die to yourself.
- You will be resurrected and have the fire as well as the water.
- Baptism means you submit to the death, burial, and resurrection of Jesus Christ.
- The Father designates the seats on each side of Jesus at the table.
- Promotion and position come from the Lord.
- When you die to yourself, you will be resurrected, then walk in fire and authority.
- You will be completely handed over to the authority of the kingdom.

DISCUSSION:

Can you submit to this because this is what is important? Regarding rewards, the Father gives out the rewards, and whoever sits in those seats of honor, the Father is going to decide. We can do what we should do: the cup and the baptisms. However, in the end, the disciples deserted Him, and Jesus had to call them together. He said, "Yet it shall not be so among you; but whoever desires to become great among you, let him be your servant. And whoever desires to be first among you, let him be your slave—just as the Son of Man did not come to be served, but to serve, and to give His life a ransom for many." (Matthew 20:26-28).

- ❖ The baptism and drinking of that cup will make you a servant to everyone. You are an example.
  - You are the one that if no one else is going to do it, you do it.

- You don't wait for someone else to initiate it; you do it.
- A true servant is a leader because a servant will go and do it.
- A person who has genuinely become a CEO or President of a company, if you read their history, they started by themselves.
- They did everything themselves until they could find people to implement and help serve in whatever capacity.
- When the company got big, that person took on people with the same vision, purpose, and plan and taught them how to serve. Everyone became servants.
- Companies excel because this is their model.

❖ Unfortunately, when companies become big, they focus on money, which becomes the driving factor. Companies will then disappear or be taken over by someone else.

- Some people push themselves into positions which happens with Christians who are weak and, in their souls, misunderstand authority.
- They feel entitled and want things now, unlike those who have walked with God for many years and sacrificed and did it themselves. They will take any opportunity to be thrust forward when they are not ready.
- Many opportunities are not God, and people's agendas and motives are wrong.
- For people who want to get recognized and popular, it ends up being a false thing. Not every opportunity that presents itself is God.

- You need to drink from the cup and be baptized with the baptisms, and the Lord will reward you for diligently seeking Him.
- Let the Father designate where you sit at the Marriage Supper of the Lamb.
- What is important is submission to authority and the kingdom of God.

Have you experienced an opportunity that was not of God?

____

____

____

____

CHAPTER 4

By What Authority?

Now when He came into the temple, the chief priests and the elders of the people confronted Him as He was teaching, and said, "By what authority are You doing these things? And who gave You this authority?"

—Matthew 21:23

DISCUSSION:

When Jesus came into the temple, the chief priests and the elders confronted Him as He was teaching and said, by what authority are you doing these things? These people were in charge but starting to feel left out. Jesus was doing all these things as the crowds followed Him, and they were not in the synagogues. It was probably hurting the Pharisees, scribes, and temple priests financially. Judas was a disciple who kept the treasury bag for Jesus, meaning they took and accepted offerings. If the people were not going to the synagogue anymore, they were not giving, and the temple's and synagogues' economic situation would be affected. All the teaching and studies they did in the temple and synagogues were not being enforced. Who gave authority to Jesus to do these things? The chief priests and the elders were losing control of the people. So, the chief priests and elders assumed that Jesus was off track because the people did not respect the Pharisees' authority under Moses.

Why were the chief priests and elders contesting Jesus?

____

____

____

____

SENT OR WENT

❖ **<u>JOHN 17:18:</u>**

As You sent Me into the world, I also have sent them into the world.

- Jesus came to fulfill all the laws and become the New Covenant.
- The crowds followed Jesus' teachings and miracles, but Jesus was continually contested about His authority and who gave it to Him.
- You also will encounter a religious organization or activity contesting you, so you better know you were sent.

❖ Suppose you are in a church or religious organization that is compromised according to how it is set up scripturally to operate.

- In that case, you will have to be sent there to help, help the pastor, or help the minister do what they are called to do and bring them up to that level. If they do not accept your help, then there is no reason for you to be there.

- Jesus was not welcome at the synagogue anymore because of the demon-possessed.
- The Pharisees didn't know they were demon-possessed.
- Jesus would go there, and the demons would start to manifest.
- Jesus would heal people, and miracles happened.
- The Pharisees' thought Jesus was undermining their establishment and authority.
- The Pharisees were under manipulation and control.

What were the Pharisees operating in?

____

____

____

____

HEAVEN OR MEN

❖ **<u>MATTHEW 21:24-25:</u>**

But Jesus answered and said to them, "I also will ask you one thing which if you tell Me, I likewise will tell you by what authority I do these things. The baptism of John—where was it from? From heaven or from men?" And they reasoned among themselves, saying, "If we say, 'From heaven,' He will say to us, 'Why then did you not believe him?' But if we say, 'From men,' we fear the multitude, for all count John as a prophet."

- Jesus was sent by God.
- John was a forerunner and did everything he was supposed to do.
- The works manifesting by Jesus were from the Father.
- Jesus was submissive to the Father.
- The Holy Spirit is now on the earth and came on the day of Pentecost.
- The Holy Spirit is upon us and in us.
- We are supposed to submit to the Holy Spirit and do the works of the Father as they manifest through us.

DISCUSSION:

Jesus asked them a question, but He gave them the answer by asking them the question. He showed that people operate in authority, and many who came before Him operated in that authority. One of these people was John the Baptist. When asked about him, they reasoned among themselves; "if we say from Heaven, He will say, then why did you not believe him? But if you speak from men, it says we fear the multitude for all count John as a prophet." Jesus knew they were stuck, and they answered, "we don't know." Rebuffing them, Jesus said, "Neither will I tell you by what authority I do these things."

- **<u>JOHN 16:13-14:</u>**

  However, when He, the Spirit of truth, has come, He will guide you into all truth; for He will not speak on His own *authority,* but whatever He hears He

will speak; and He will tell you things to come. He will glorify Me, for He will take of what is Mine and declare *it* to you.

- We now realize that the Holy Spirit is a servant too. Jesus said the Holy Spirit will not speak on His own when He does come.
- The Holy Spirit will only speak what the Father says, and He will only do what the Father is doing. It will be like Jesus when He was there.
- Authority is recognized in a ministry by this example by speaking by the Holy Spirit.
- When you operate, you do things by the Holy Spirit.
- People will see if you are operating by the Holy Spirit or if it is trial and error or random.
- Everything is already established in Heaven—it is called absolute truth.
- God's throne is made of absolute truth, and there are layers on His throne. In Psalm 89, David talks about this.
- God is sitting on His throne, and it has layers of righteousness, justice, and truth. Angels are His faithfulness, and they surround His throne.

What are we supposed to be doing now on the earth?

____

____

____

____

KNOWN BY THEIR FRUIT

❖ **MATTHEW 7:16 NLT:**

You can identify them by their fruit, that is, by the way they act. Can you pick grapes from thornbushes or figs from thistles?

- There are things in Heaven that if you can establish on earth, the kingdom would automatically start to come in and manifest.
- You must resolve in your heart that you are under authority, which is rigged in your favor if you do what you are told.
- God taught us through Jesus Christ and all the apostles that you will know them by their fruit. Because of the fruit, you will see and identify that God is with a person.
- It will be easy and obvious to know people by their fruit.
- You must become like a child in your faith.
- It is hard for someone in their head to receive from the Lord and walk with God supernaturally.
- Place yourself in a position to hear from God and be willing to do what He says.
- The entitlement type of mentality will seek their own agenda.

How are we to be known by others?

____

____

____

____

ENTITLEMENT VS SERVANTHOOD

❖ **LUKE 22:26 NLT:**

But among you it will be different. Those who are the greatest among you should take the lowest rank, and the leader should be like a servant.

- Opportunists will say if you do this for me, I will do this for you. It is all entitlement, and this generation is where people feel like they can have this even if it took forty years for another person to achieve it.
- They want things in a short amount of time, and they do not want to pay their dues.
- People like the Pharisees or denominations are in control and manipulate and take advantage of others because they have stars in their eyes. They want to get attention and focus on only certain parts of the message.
- The religious don't want to hear about brokenness and repentance.
- They have not been taught about paying the price and dying to self.
- They do not want the powerful words in the Bible about perseverance and persecution.
- How about obeying God?

- How about being a servant to all and never expecting God to pay you back as in promoting you?

DISCUSSION:

That happened to me. I had to stay thirty years in a servant place and not be promoted. When I could be promoted, the Lord would say, "No, you are not doing that." I would have to turn it down, or I was going to be disobedient. People do this, and they think it is okay. However, not every opportunity presented to them is of God—it is actually a trap, which is why people get off track. It happens when people are getting off and operating wrongly. I used to think it must be God if it sounds good and it's a ministry opportunity, but they were often incorrect, and it got me off. I remember the Lord appearing to me once because I had done this. I had assumed the opportunity was Him but had not asked, sought, or even given Him time to speak to me by the Spirit.

The Lord appeared to me, coming into my room and waking me up. He was very upset with me. God does get upset with you because He loves those who obey Him. He said, "If you love Me, you obey Me," and I had not obeyed Him. I had become an opportunist and assumed He would give me a fast track. I was assuming that I was entitled to promotion, but I was not entitled to promotion. He told me He let me know that I did not have permission to do what I was asked to do, that I accepted it, and that I was never to do that again until I checked in with Him. Alarmingly, He walked away and wouldn't even talk to me. He has since visited me, and everything is fine, but He had to take that stand.

❖ You need to stay true, even if it hurts, and even if you do not get promoted right away.

- Jesus said to be a servant to everyone.
- God is working all things out for you.
- You are going to be sent, not just went.
- Not every opportunity that comes to you is God.
- If you follow the Lord and do ministry, you must be a servant willing to take the low road.
- You may have to say no to a great opportunity because people have bad intentions.

Is everything that comes before you what God wants you to do?

____

____

____

____

THE NARROW WAY

Jesus is asking if He will find obedience when He comes? He did not answer that question because He will let us decide how that outcome will be. Is He going to find faith on the earth? He is with us because we are going to be obedient. We love Him, and so we are going to obey Him.

- **<u>MATTHEW 7:13-14:</u>**

  Enter by the narrow gate; for wide *is* the gate and broad *is* the way that leads to destruction, and there are many who go in by it. Because narrow *is* the gate and difficult *is* the way which leads to life, and there are few who find it.

  - Many are going the wrong way, and there is a narrow way, but few find it.
  - Many choose the road of destruction, which is wide, and many find that Jesus said, "When I come back, will I find faith in the earth?"
  - Jesus is asking if He will find obedience when He comes? He did not answer that question because He will let us decide how that outcome will be.
  - Is He going to find faith on the earth? He is with us because we are going to be obedient. We love Him, and so we are going to obey Him.
  - We need to hear from the Lord.
  - Most people have unrealistic expectations about what is going to happen.
  - You do not understand authority when you expect something like an entitlement where God will do this for you.
  - God does not have to do anything for you at all.
  - God cannot go against His Word.
  - You cannot pressure God when it looks like He must do something for you.

- ❖ Sometimes, God did not do what I wanted because He is running the show, and I am not. You won't do that if you want to get anywhere with Him, and I have learned not to do that.

  - People have gotten into trouble because they say things God has said, but God never said that. They say something and then go down the road, which is not the right road.
  - Then those people must backtrack, and it is uncomfortable. They must return from the cave because it was a dead end.
  - Part of kingdom principles is that we need to hear from God.
  - We need to know His Word.
  - If you do not know what to do, do not do anything until you hear from God.

DISCUSSION:

I felt called from the beginning that I was supposed to start a school and was called to be a teacher, so I wanted to be in media. I wanted to be a teacher and stick to what God had told me, but it did not come easy. I had to get my own studio and start my own school. I could not fit in anywhere else, and God said, "I want you to do this the way I tell you to do it correctly, so I want you to start your own." So, we have had to start our own everything. No one with power and influence came and stepped in to help me. I had to pray it out and do it myself. The bottom line was that the Holy Spirit, my wife, and I prayed it through, and then our staff. Many people do not realize that God must do it. Abraham would not take any help from the king of Sodom because he said, "I don't want you to say later that you made Abraham rich" (Genesis 14:22-23). I believe that this will happen to you.

- Don't take it personally if people are not there to help and serve you.
- God will send those people to you, but you may have to start yourself.
- The reward comes from doing it on your own, and you get good people and the right people to help.
- The kingdom principle is that God is in authority.
- God is not asking you for your opinion or your input in anything.
- God is telling you, "This is how We do things, and this is My plan for your life."

PRAYER

The Holy Spirit wants to implement God's plan right now, and all the angels are sent to you to perform His will in your life. The angels already know what you are supposed to be doing, so you need to be submissive and hear from the Holy Spirit. I believe that you are receiving from the Father in the name of Jesus. May you hear His voice clearly and that you are given power, mercy, and grace to obey the Holy Spirit. May you take baby steps in the right direction and follow the Lord's will to walk into your destiny in Jesus' name. Amen.

CHAPTER 5

Manifestations of Evil Spirits

When He had come to the other side, to the country of the Gergesenes there met Him two demon-possessed men, *coming out of the tombs exceedingly fierce, so that no one could pass that way. And suddenly they cried out, saying, "What have we to do with You, Jesus, You Son of God? Have You come here to torment us before the time?"*

—Matthew 8:28-29

DISCUSSION:

When Jesus showed up, the demons knew who He was. In the Old Testament, satan's name is barely mentioned, and there were few demon-possessed people or demonic activity. Interestingly, when Jesus began to walk the earth in the New Testament, you see manifestations of evil spirits. Jesus showed up in the synagogue, and a man started manifesting and confronting Him, so Jesus confronted that demon and cast it out in front of all of them. When you walk in the authority of the kingdom, you will confront devils. Jesus would just show up, stand up, and preach the Word. He did not come to wrestle demons.

❖ Jesus came and read the Scriptures and taught the people. Jesus had authority, and He was sent.

- The demons were there a long time but suddenly became apparent when encountering kingdom authority.
- The demons came out of hiding.
- Jesus was asked to teach, and He read from the scroll of Scriptures.
- After Jesus read, He taught them, and the demons got stirred up.
- Jesus healed people, and miracles happened.
- The demons were there the whole time, but Jesus' temperature was much hotter.
- Jesus tells us not to be lukewarm.
- We must have good teaching and hear and obey it; that is how faith comes.

What happens when you walk in kingdom authority?

____

____

____

____

FAITH COMES BY HEARING

❖ **ROMANS 10:17:**

So then faith *comes* by hearing, and hearing by the word of God.

- Hearing the Word causes us to believe, and we act. Action is obedience, and the fruit or the manifestation of faith is an act.
- We must act it out, obeying the Word. We hear it and then do something about it.
- Demons are driven out by who you are.
- You show up, and it stirs things up.
- You do not understand your environment, you feel rejected, and things get harder when starting to walk in kingdom authority.
- You become hot, the demons get stirred up, and you are uncomfortable.
- The demons know that you will address them and cast them out.

DISCUSSION:

You must understand that your daily activity will alert the demons while gaining authority and knowing who you are. The minute you leave your house and get into your car, the demons are wondering where you are going and what you will do because the Holy Spirit is leading you. While you are out, you will encounter people who are bound by devils, and they do not even know it. There are all kinds of demonic activity entrenched in establishments like the grocery store. It does not matter whether you think you are effective; you just want to go to the store and buy some milk. However, the devils are concerned with what you know and will do. If you have checked with the Holy Spirit, then a demon considers you a threat to their control and manipulation. Be mindful that even if you think you are not effective, you are effective. It is based on what you understand, what you take away from what you hear, and what you have implemented into your life.

- You are becoming a person like the Apostle Paul; he was changed because he was caught up.
  - Paul understood authority and the body of Christ.
  - You must be saturated and filled with teaching on authority and demons.
  - The demons assume that you are going to cast them out and that you will witness to the people.
  - They assume that you are not going to back off.
  - The demons will come at you, and they will want to prevent you from going places.
  - If you go places and you are successful, the demons do not want you to talk to anybody.
  - The demons do not want you to tell the truth about the gospel because they will lose control over people.

- What happens is people will see you, and that demon will get them to think terrible things and feel terrible things, then the person will reject you because they feel rejected.
  - They feel rejected because of what they are walking in and the spirit on them and in them.
  - When the demons encounter you, they are going to manifest. When they manifest, they have revealed themselves because demons cannot shut up.

- The demons feel very uncomfortable around you and cannot sit there and be quiet. So, they will do all kinds of things.
- You cannot feel rejected or take it as the truth—the demons are reacting.
- Jesus had this happen to Him everywhere He went.

❖ Unfortunately, some people in the church are entrenched in their souls. They may be born again and spirit-filled, but they have been influenced by their mind, will, and emotions.

- Peter was able to speak according to the Spirit, and then he was rebuked when he spoke according to evil spirits as well, be aware that the same is in the church today (Matthew 16:23).
- Jesus addressed Peter as speaking by satan.
- Jesus had to tell Peter to shut up.
- You are going to have to walk in love and understanding.
- Do not accept rejection from an evil spirit; when people reject you, they reject Jesus Christ.

❖ **2 CORINTHIANS 10:4-6**

For the weapons of our warfare *are* not carnal but mighty in God for pulling down strongholds, casting down arguments and every high thing that exalts itself against the knowledge of God, bringing every thought into captivity to the obedience of Christ, and being ready to punish all disobedience when your obedience is fulfilled.

- Paul talked about this warfare as anything that exalts itself above the knowledge of God, bringing it into captivity to the obedience of Christ.
- Your love walk is not a gooey feeling; *God loves me, and I want to be saturated in His power, and I love everyone.*
- If you love people, you tell them the truth, which will cause a firestorm.
- Sometimes you get hit with a bee's nest.
- You are the one who is called to do it.
- Jesus caused division wherever He went by speaking the truth.
- Paul caused division and riots everywhere he went.
- Paul was thrown in jail, and everywhere he went, he caused problems.
- He did not cause problems, but it was for righteousness' sake.
- You are right, and you represent righteousness.
- You are going somewhere because God is sending you.
- He is sending you to cause a confrontation and a war because that is what happened with Jesus.
- Jesus did not come to start fighting with the Pharisees; they found Him, but He always spoke the truth by the Father.

How are demons driven out?

____

____

____

____

DISCUSSION:

The movements we have seen in the Spirit have turned into denominations and become brick and mortar. They started by the power of the Spirit. It is important to know that you, too, can move by the Spirit. We may not feel called to a certain church, and you want to teach so you can have a bible study in your home every week. You are not competing against a church because you are creating a safe place for people to come to know the love of Christ and become free.

GET LIT UP IN THE SPIRIT

- **<u>EPHESIANS 4:15-16:</u>**

  But, speaking the truth in love, may grow up in all things into Him who is the head—Christ—from whom the whole body, joined and knit together by what every joint supplies, according to the effective working by which every part does its share causes growth of the body for the edifying of itself in love.

  - The Fivefold Ministry is to build up and equip the church to go out and minister to the unsaved.
  - The church is to be ambassadors representing Jesus Christ to the world but knows that confrontation is inevitable.
  - If devils don't know who you are and they don't manifest, I would be disappointed.
  - The devil is still here, hiding behind the scenes and operating through people. We are wrestling against them, so we need to take them out.

- Many people are ignorant and won't understand that they are being used or controlled.
- You need to get lit up in the spirit and be powerful.
- You need to get caught on fire, stay hot, and be just like Jesus.
- The devils could not just sit quietly and shut up. They were getting hit by the holiness and the righteousness of God.
- They were being judged, and they were feeling it.
- The body of Christ needs to be here, so everywhere you go, you are hot, and the evil spirits know who you are.
- Many times, it takes a whole weekend of preaching, teaching, and praying before there is not one devil within the proximity of the building.

Why don't the devils sit quietly?

____

____

____

____

PRAYER

Father, thank You in the name of Jesus for teaching us about operating in kingdom authority. We want to walk in our authority and be like Jesus wherever He went, doing good and healing everyone, the oppressed of the devil. Thank you

that Jesus did not have to look for devils. As Jesus ministered to the people, the devils would manifest. Thank You, Lord, for the special anointing and the power of the Holy Spirit that breaks, yokes and drives out the enemy. Thank You for this impartation from Heaven that I know who I am and walk in kingdom authority, in Jesus' name. Amen

CHAPTER 6

Kingdom Transfer

And Jesus came and spoke to them, saying, "All authority has been given to Me in heaven and on earth. Go therefore and make disciples of all the nations, baptizing them in the name of the Father and of the Son and of the Holy Spirit, teaching them to observe all things that I have commanded you; and lo, I am with you always, even to the end of the age. Amen.

—Matthew 28:18-20

DISCUSSION:

Jesus taught us about the kingdom and how it operates, but we need to understand how to do this in everyday life. Jesus told His disciples that He would go away, and they would have to carry on advancing the kingdom. The whole idea of the kingdom was that it was transferrable from what Jesus was doing to what the disciples were assigned to do. We have this commission and authority that what is in Heaven is on the earth. We are commissioned to baptize people in the name of the Father, the Son, and the Holy Spirit. We are commissioned to teach them until the end of the age.

❖ This commission that Jesus gave us has given us full authority. The commission causes everything to bow and acknowledge that Jesus is Lord. The commission gives authority to go to every nation, make disciples, and baptize them in the name of the Father, the Son, and the Holy Spirit.

- Jesus said to teach the people and observe all the things commanded.
- You must study to show yourself approved.
- You must realize that you have the authority given by God through Jesus Christ.
- You are to study, meditate, and pray out in the Spirit all the mysteries.
- You must concentrate on the fact that God has sent you, and He has already prepared the way for you.
- Everything will work out no matter where you are sent, and God will be with you in a mighty way.

What have we been commissioned to do?

____

____

____

____

BE ESTABLISHED AND MADE COMPLETE

❖ **2 CORINTHIANS 13:9-10:**

For we are glad when we are weak and you are strong. And this also we pray, that you may be made complete. Therefore I write these things being absent, lest being present I should use sharpness, according to the authority which the Lord has given me for edification and not for destruction.

- The Lord gave Paul authority for their edification and not for their destruction. Paul was under authority, but we are also given authority to manage people.
- The Spirit of the Lord is doing that today among the body through the Fivefold Ministry.
- As you mature in the Lord, He shows you what you are called to do, and you will walk in that authority also. The authority will create boundaries.
- The authority will create an atmosphere for growth and accountability.
- There is freedom and liberty where the Spirit of the Lord is present.
- You must yield to the Holy Spirit and not be bound and go your own way. We are to be governed by the Spirit. We are to walk in the Spirit.
- If you are not yielding and obeying in the Spirit, those in authority will need to address those issues in your life.
- Human nature needs boundaries and discipline that are healthy and not restricted.

- God loves those that He disciplines, and He disciplines those He loves.

What does authority do?

____

____

____

____

ACCOUNTABILITY AND MATURITY

DISCUSSION:

Many people need to be held accountable because it helps them stay in there and do the right thing, whereas normally, they would not. We all need each other. As Jesus taught His disciples, He made known to them when they were in doubt or walking in fear, or if they were in disobedience. When the disciples saw Jesus, after He appeared to them, after being raised from the dead, it says some of them doubted. Jesus had been with them for three and a half years, and this would seem foreign that they doubted or feared.

❖ **<u>EPHESIANS 4:13 NLT</u>**

This will continue until we all come to such unity of our faith and knowledge of God's Son that we will be mature in the Lord, measuring up to the full and complete standard of Christ.

- The Spirit of the Lord reveals our human behavior and brings freedom.
- The Spirit of the Lord brings truth; it brings reality.
- We need to be able to self-govern our own lives.
- We can listen to the Spirit and do the right thing without being told what to do.
- The Lord wants us to be further along than where we are.

Why should you be accountable?

____

____

____

____

DIFFERENT ASPECTS OF AUTHORITY

❖ **<u>TITUS 2:15 NLT:</u>**

You must teach these things and encourage the believers to do them. You have the authority to correct them when necessary, so don't let anyone disregard what you say.

- There are different aspects of authority.
- One is to exhort, rebuke, and let no one despise you because you are young or for whatever reason.
- You are reminded to be subject to rulers and those in authority by obeying and being ready for every good work.

- If you act appropriately, even at your job, you obey and are submissive; then people will be attracted to you and want to know why you have the attitude you do.
- Do your job and do not complain and your boss will notice you.
- The Holy Spirit will cause you to be a good witness to others.
- Be submissive to authority and do a good job.
- Yielding to the Spirit will cause you to go beyond what you are asked to do.

❖ Another aspect of authority is in prayer for intercession. You become very aggressive in prayer. The Spirit of God will want you to deal with a sharpness and an authority to intercede for someone else.

- The attitude will be that you are not letting go until you get an answer for someone else.
- Authority is used in prayer for intercession.
- You are going to go beyond what you can go on your own.
- The Spirit of God wants to intercede for someone who cannot do it alone.
- You must come in and pick up the burden and be aggressive.
- Those people's lives are in the balance, and the Lord wants to come back for a Bride that does not have spots or wrinkles.
- There should be intercession for those who are lukewarm and falling away.

- There is an authority and a dominion taking place for another person.

❖ There is authority to drive out the enemy of God with our authority in the kingdom. When people are bound and have allowed the enemy to come in, or are negligent, or ignorant about what satan is doing, you need to establish your authority in the Spirit and understand how to operate and drive out devils.

- You need to be very aggressive.
- The Spirit of God is powerful, and He is very protective of believers because God has assigned them to Him.
- There is authority in the kingdom, and it is also given to leadership.

❖ The Fivefold Ministry has authority as well. When we speak, we should speak as though we are speaking the very words of God.

- The authority of the kingdom should be upon us.
- We should be speaking not for someone's destruction.
- We should be speaking for edification, correction, and building up.

What are some different aspects of authority?

____

____

____

____

THE KINGDOM IS ADVANCING RAPIDLY

❖ **ROMANS 8:14:**

For as many as are led by the Spirit of God, these are sons of God.

- The power of God is advancing powerfully.
- Many people are waiting on God to move them somehow. But in reality, you are supposed to be led by the Spirit.
- God is not going to make anybody do anything. Some people think that God will forcibly come in and show them or be aggressive. Realistically, that is not the way God is.
- When you are hungry and seek God and ask Him for help, He will come in and help, but you need to participate with the Spirit of the Lord.
- The Spirit wants to give us everything we need to do this life.
- The Spirit gives us gifts and the ability to produce fruit in the keeping with repentance.
- The angels and the Spirit of God want the kingdom to advance and grow.
- People need to engage and get involved with the Spirit of God by praying, fasting, and seeking God.

❖ **ISAIAH 10:27 KJV:**

And it shall come to pass in that day, that his burden shall be taken away from off thy shoulder, and his yoke from off thy neck, and the yoke shall be destroyed because of the anointing.

- The kingdom wants to advance, and the anointing wants to break yokes.
- God wants to heal people and deliver people.
- We must allow the Spirit to have His way by actively participating and asking God to use us.
- Moves of God happen through prayer and intercession.
- The Spirit is going to come in and build you up.
- There will be a powerful time of being disciplined and mentored.
- You will start walking in authority and become mature and accountable.
- Then God will trust you with even greater things

How do you rapidly advance the kingdom of God?

____

____

____

____

ESTABLISHING THE KINGDOM

❖ **JUDE 1:20 NLT:**

But you, dear friends, must build each other up in the most holy faith, pray in the power of the Holy Spirit.

- One of the most important things you can do is intercede by praying in the Spirit and allowing your spirit to pray out the mysteries.
- You will discover that this needs to be a lifelong discipline.
- You need to get used to praying in the Spirit as often as you can.
- When we pray in the Spirit, we are building ourselves up.
- We establish the kingdom of God inside us and speak it out.
- When established, the angels are going to help you outwardly.
- You will get strong in faith, the Word of God, and the Spirit; it will
- come forth.
- You will start to feel aggressive and will not take no for an answer.

❖ Things are going to flip. Jesus was anointed and went around doing good and healing everyone the devil oppressed (Acts 10:38). It became very forcible and was advancing, but it was not because He was waiting on the Spirit to do this for Him.

- Jesus actively engaged, grew up, built Himself up, and matured.
- Jesus became anointed by God to go forth.
- Let God borrow your voice, igniting you and causing you to speak boldly.
- Spend time praying and meditating, and then God will borrow your life. God wants to minister through you.
- The enemy will back off, and darkness will be pushed back.

- You become motivated and moved by the Holy Spirit.
- You have allowed the process to mature you.
- Become aggressive; Engage the Holy Spirit, and the kingdom and the angels will operate for you.
- When you pray, you will feel aggressive toward intercession.
- You will drive out devils, protect people, and cause boundaries to be made in the Spirit.
- When you pray, you may feel warfare.
- You may be standing in the gap for someone else when you pray.
- You may be praying for people to be more accountable, and they need light on what is going on in their lives.
- The kingdom is advancing through you, and God will change your territory and send you to different places to establish authority there.

What are the different ways you may be praying?

____

____

____

____

CHAPTER 7

Territorial Authority

Because you say, I am rich, have become wealthy, and have need of nothing'—and do not know that you are wretched, miserable, poor, blind and naked—
—Revelation 3:17

DISCUSSION:

You will discover the system down here in this kingdom of darkness as you travel from city to city; you will find that there are different atmospheres and a different feel about things, and you notice that people are a bit different. The Apostle John told the Laodiceans who thought that they were rich, but they were poor. They thought they were well dressed, but they were naked. Paul wrote to the seven churches in Northern Turkey that they had succumbed to the spirit operating in those cities. He addressed false doctrine and told them they needed to repent. As you travel from town to town, city to city, or state to state, a sort of character or personality of that city could be referred to as a spirit. You can find certain traits, and you can feel them.

- **<u>EPHESIANS 6:12 AMP:</u>**

  For our struggle is not against flesh and blood [contending only with physical opponents], but against the rulers, against the powers, against the world forces of this [present] darkness, against the spiritual *forces* of wickedness in the heavenly (supernatural) *places*.

  - Working in the airlines taught me to identify and recognize territories, different domains, principalities, and authorities and the principalities of the power of the air.
  - You need to investigate and understand these things, not ignore them and hope they go away.
  - You must understand your authority in the Spirit and the warfare you will go through.
  - You need to resist these personalities and don't succumb to them.

- It is often better when someone comes and visits from another area because they are not affected by this, and they can help. Traveling ministers are effective when they come into other territories and can recognize and identify territorial spirits.

  - Evangelists, apostles, prophets, and teachers come from different areas and can see and address things people living there are unaware of.
  - Paul did this when he traveled and understood authority in the kingdom and the warfare.
  - You can learn how to deal with different atmospheres and know how

to help people.

- If people want help, you can help them, but if they do not see it, then it is more complicated.
- If you do not grasp these principles, you will be overcome by things you should not have to experience.
- Many people do not understand what they are up against in this area.
- When you move to a different city, some things will cease, but others will come. Every city has entities assigned to it.
- Jesus experienced this in every city because demon spirits would come and confront Him, saying, "Have you come to torment us before our time?"
- The demons Jesus encountered would say, "Do not send us out of the area" because they had established their kingdoms there.

❖ The region's higher-up principalities, powers, and authorities confronted Jesus. There were many smaller subjects, demons under those doing the dirty work—like worker bees. When you come into a territory, you confront those demons in higher authority.

- When you address the higher-in-authority ones, all the others will fall. You take out the giant, so to speak.
- Individuals who are sent can create a group of people who agree in prayer and stick together, and do not allow these spirits to divide them.
- Right now, we are establishing our territories all over the world.

Where do territorial spirits live?

____

____

____

____

TAKE BACK TERRITORY

DISCUSSION:

When people gather and pray in unity, they can push back the darkness, and it becomes an outpost and a command center for that area. As it grows and is kept pure, you take back more territory for the kingdom of God. The Lord has different ways of doing this. Sometimes He moves you from where you grew up because of the familiar spirits that influenced you when you grew up there. It can be difficult to overcome them. I encountered this when I would come back and visit from college; the spirit I grew up with would try to control me. Even though I didn't live there anymore, I could still feel it. It was because it was familiar to me, and so I had to get away to deal with all of that.

❖ **<u>MARK 3:27:</u>**

No one can enter a strong man's house and plunder his goods, unless he first binds the strong man. And then he will plunder his house.

- People do not know that a demonic spirit is not part of who they are as a person because it has become part of their characteristics or their personality.
- If you are assigned to a certain city or territory, you must allow the fruit of the Spirit to manifest and allow the Spirit of God to dictate who you are and to be established in Christ.
- Most people must move away from their parents and from that territory.
- There are assignments against your bloodline; if you are in another place, you can establish your authority and deal with these things.
- You need to name and label the spirit controlling you in an area.
- You need to recognize that the spirit has no power over you.
- You need to grow and be established in your authority and let the Spirit of God dictate who you are.
- You will find that a lot of your personality that you thought was you is not you because of familiar spirits in your area.
- When you move to another area, you become another person.
- You can become well versed in atmospheres, environments, and different governmental boundaries in the spirit.

Why do people have to move away from where they were born?

____

____

____

____

TAKE THE GIANT OUT

❖ **1 SAMUEL 16:23:**

And so it was, whenever the spirit from God was upon Saul, that David would take a harp ad play it with his hand. Then Saul would become refreshed and well and the distressing spirit would depart from him.

- Knowing those territories and people responding to what is happening behind the scenes is important.
- We are all called and are supposed to have a personal relationship with Jesus.
- David was trained in the field, watching sheep. He trained for accuracy with his slingshot, and he played his harp. He was a loner, but he learned how to do warfare because when he went to battle, he could take out the giant instantly.
- David learned as he played the flute that he could go to different atmospheres and function by taking the giant out.
- David did not hesitate; the demons left Saul when he played the harp.
- People need to be trained and established to function no matter their territory. You don't want to be paralyzed when you are at your job or other places.
- When you go anywhere, you do not want to become perturbed or get off balance just because you feel something changed in your spirit, and you don't know why.
- When you feel irritated, it is because you are confronting something and are supposed to take it out.

- God will send you places, and you will be ready to operate in any atmosphere.
- The Lord can build you up, train you, and you can step into kingdom authority, so wherever He sends you, you can change the atmosphere and the territory because you do warfare, and you don't budge.

How do you change the atmosphere or territory you are in?

____

____

____

____

PARALLEL WORLD

❖ **GENESIS 6:6-7 NIV:**

The LORD regretted that he had made human beings on the earth, and his heart was deeply troubled." So the LORD said, I will wipe from the face of the earth the human race I have created—and with them the animals, the birds and the creatures that move along the ground—for I regret that I have made them."

- There are entities all over the earth, and a whole race of beings are disembodied from the flood.
- They do not have a body, but they are on the earth and close to where they were before the flood.

- It is not time for them to be judged yet; even though the judgment has been made, they are allowed to roam the earth, and their torment is coming.
- These entities do not want to leave the area that they are in. They begged Jesus not to send them out of the area and not to torment them before their time.

❖ When we accept that there is a parallel world and beings are here that have been judged by God, but the angels have not come to take them away and incarcerate them, then with kingdom authority, you will drive them out—displacing them. They need to be pushed out from where they are at; that is, eviction and forceful.

- When people do not make decisions, evil spirits get them to compromise and be indecisive.
- Jesus just drives out the demons, but they wanted to stay in their territory.
- The demons want to get back into people and have a body again.
- The demons need to have an expression in this realm because they are disembodied.
- People need to be trained not to allow demons to get into people.
- Dealing with devils can be in prayer and walking in the knowledge of who you are.
- You understand that you are in a specific territory where there are

good and evil forces working around you.

❖ **MARK 16:17:**

And these signs will follow those who believe: In My name they will cast out demons; they will speak with new tongues;

- You have authority that Jesus Christ gave you through His name and blood and you use that authority to drive out demons.
- You must enforce and exercise your authority yourself.
- You must be prayerful when their demons manifest and be sharp and quick to the point.
- Do not allow demons to steal the show in any way or to manifest.
- You stop the manifestations, and you do not argue with them.
- You tell the demons that they must leave.
- Demons operate in a cloaked mode, not being visible and doing sneaky things.
- When things happen, and you sense in your spirit that it is an evil spirit, you need to address it.
- Interference with demons can happen with electronics and other things. They may break or slow down. Or it could be the behaviors of people.
- You need to label things, address them spiritually as an entity, and drive them out.
- You need to pray, intercede, and be quick and to the point, so things do not manifest.
- When praying for the sick, you should bind the devil and drive them out. Forbid the devil to manifest.

- If people are having symptoms, address the symptoms as well.
- An evil spirit's presence can cause sickness. Other times people just need healing.
- Jesus healed those who the devil oppressed.
- Jesus rebuked sickness, drove out the devil, and healed everyone that was oppressed by the devil.

Where did the disembodied spirits now on the earth come from?

____

____

____

____

ANOINTING BREAKS THE YOKE

❖ **<u>MATTHEW 11:29-30:</u>**

Take My yoke upon you and learn from Me, for I am gentle and lowly in heart, and you will find rest for your souls. For My yoke *is* easy and My burden is light."

- The anointing upon Jesus broke the yoke and bondage off of people (Isaiah 10:27). Jesus was sent and authorized, and so are you to do the same, healing the sick and casting out devils.
- Jesus has commissioned you to do that. We have already been sent, so we do not have to wait for anything.

- When I met Jesus, He was a powerful personality because He was a king. He is forceful, but He is kind.
- Jesus loves people but is convinced and forceful about His Father's kingdom. No one argues with Jesus.
- When people are argumentative, they are not in repentance but in rebellion.
- When people are argumentative, they are not fully convinced.
- People who encounter the Lord are humble and want the best for everyone.
- We, as the church, need to step into our authority because the body of Christ is not where it needs to be.

How do you know people are in rebellion?

____

____

____

____

RETURN TO YOUR FIRST LOVE

DISCUSSION:

Individually we need to strengthen each other so that we can be leaders and start a movement to influence people and get them back to their first love. When Jesus visited the seven churches, He said, "I want you to return to your first love." We need to get back to the basics by having people walk in a relationship with Him and

focus on the relationship part, not just the position part. When you are in position, you emphasize all the things that the privilege of being in Christ brings, like the righteousness of God in Christ Jesus (2 Corinthians 5:21). We are holy because He is holy (1 Peter 1:16). Even though Adam and Eve had fallen that day, God came walking in the garden like He usually did. He called out to them as though nothing had happened. He knew what had happened, but He had a relationship with them.

❖ **REVELATION 2:4:**

Nevertheless I have *this* against you, that you have left your first love.

- When you walk with the Lord and have established a relationship, rebellion and pride will be gone.
- They become legalistic when a person is only walking in position and not in a relationship.
- People who do not want to be religious with all the dos and don'ts end up being religious because they have left their first love.
- Religious people do not have a relationship, only a bunch of rules.
- We need to walk in authority and in our relationship, so we are working through things and will be problem solvers.
- We will have a solution, and there will be no rebellion.
- We will not resist what God is saying and what He is doing.
- When people are rebellious and resistant to things, you will find demonic activity involved in their life.

What do religious people not have?

____

____

____

____

PRAYER

Father, I thank You for deliverance. I thank You that our eyes are seeing, and our ears are hearing what You are saying. Thank You for giving us an understanding of territorial and evil spirits and how it works. Father, thank You that the power of the Holy Spirit is so strong it is causing us to triumph over our enemies. In the name of Jesus. Amen.

CHAPTER 8

Sent to Territories

"Behold, I send an Angel before you to keep you in the way and to bring you into the place which I have prepared.

—Exodus 23:20

DISCUSSION:

God has you where you are, and if you are not supposed to be there, God will move you. You need to be in the territory you have been sent to operate in the fullness of what God has for you. When you find out where you are supposed to be and get there, the Spirit of God will help you. He is more than willing to do things in your life. You will learn to be aggressive and be established in authority. Evil spirits do not want Christians to know who they are and their authority over evil spirits. Evil spirits dread the day you realize what you are called to do and start operating in it. The easiest way to establish your authority is by meditating on the Word of God, watching what Jesus did, and being baptized in the Holy Spirit.

What do evil spirits dread?

____

____

____

____

PRAY OUT MYSTERIES

- **ACTS 2:4 NKJV:**

  And they were all filled with the Holy Spirit and began to speak with other tongues, as the Spirit gave them utterance.

  - The Holy Spirit came upon all the people in the New Testament and baptized them in the Spirit and fire.
  - There were gifts of the Spirit distributed severally as the Spirit wills.
  - One of the things that we can do is to pray in the Spirit, pray in tongues, and let the Spirit pray out the mysteries.
  - You can also ask the Holy Spirit to prophesy. Paul said to desire the greater gifts like prophesy because it edifies in a known language.
  - You need to pray that you can prophesy or interpret the tongues.
  - If you interpret your tongues, it is equivalent to prophesy because prophecy is in a known language.
  - Pray and ask the Holy Spirit to help you in your warfare by prayer and walking in authority as you pray in tongues.

- Pray in tongues and then wait and ask the Lord to give you the understanding of what you are saying—the interpretation.
- Then you will participate in an understanding, not just in the Spirit, when your mind is not fruitful.
- You are praying out the mysteries of God. You are speaking from God, not to man.
- When you prophesy, those who hear it can understand because you are speaking to them.
- When you interpret, especially in territories you have been sent to, God will give you insight into what is going on.
- You will need to prophesy when God sends you into a territory, and you need to yield to the Spirit.
- Follow this— pray in tongues, interpret it, and then prophesy. As you prophesy, you can feel things being pushed back.

DISCUSSION:

There will be times when you yield to the Spirit, and the Spirit will say things that are way beyond you, and the Spirit will address and correct things. It will affect the atmosphere, and then you will have confrontation. These evil spirits are going to throw a fit. Once you know and understand what the Spirit is saying and doing, you continue with it and push through it. Sometimes it takes years or just a few minutes for you to fully yield to the Spirit, revealing what needs to be said, so things are resolved. Then you say things and purpose not to back off. There will be times when God's path will take you into this. You will be chosen to go into war against a giant

like David did. You will be taken to a place because He trusts you, and you will be sent to free people.

- ❖ God has bigger plans because sometimes it looks like one thing, but God will do something else. When God has chosen a path, and it is hard, you must realize He is sending you because He trusts you, and you will need to do warfare to change history.

    - People often get overwhelmed and are not operating in these things, so a city, state, or country seems hard.
    - Gather and have fellowship with others and strengthen each other by praying in the Spirit, encouraging one another, and allowing the Spirit to develop strategies for your region.
    - He may have you feed people, pray for people, or just be friendly, showing the love of God.
    - People need to be trained to exercise authority in their region, pray in the Spirit, prophesy, interpret tongues, move things out of the way, and release freedom.
    - Nothing changes if you do not address things, and people stay the same.
    - When Christians fail, it makes God look bad—they do not understand their authority and how to operate in it.
    - Let the Spirit teach you, and let the Spirit address things.
    - Do not ignore things; if something is wrong, do something about it.

What happens when you pray in tongues?

____

____

____

____

WHAT WE PERMIT

❖ **MATTHEW 16:19:**

And I will give you the keys of the kingdom of heaven, and whatever you bind on earth will be bound in heaven, and whatever you loose on earth will be loosed in heaven.

- When we see that something in Heaven is not happening on the earth, we are to pray that God's will come to the earth as it is in Heaven.
- It is disturbing that if we allow things, they will be allowed. It is our fault when things go wrong here, and no one likes to admit it.
- The church is ineffective because it does not understand its authority and must change things.
- The church is always on duty, and we have authority, but it backed off, and many things were never supposed to happen.
- Many things happen on the earth because the church is not doing her job and not standing up.
- When we walk in authority, we help everyone around us, and the next generation.

- The devil does not want to give up the authority or the territory that he has been given.
- The devil will not cooperate in any way, and he will be very hard and rebellious.
- You need to seek God and get the Spirit of reality on you and the environment of Heaven.
- You must continually saturate yourself to see things through the other realm. Then you can know and rightly divide and discern things correctly and know if it is not right.

❖ When I was in Heaven, what I saw disturbed me because the enemy understands human behavior, makes believers feel worthless, and robs them. The enemy prevents believers from resisting them, knowing that if the church woke up and operated in authority, they would not be able to do anything.

- It is because of the body of Christs's lukewarm condition here that things are happening.
- When you add value and worth to people and preach the good news, it builds them up to where they resist the enemy and discern rightly.
- When you discern, you address evil spirits and take a stand in your authority.
- You need to mature and set boundaries.
- If you are sent, then all the things you need for life and godliness have already been provided through these promises.

- What you need to do right now is get right with the Spirit of God, operate in your authority, and establish your relationship with God where you know your value. You know you are called; you know you are sent, and you prophesy to your world. Then you meditate on the Word of God, and it shows you what God is saying.

    - You establish yourself in your territory, and the evil spirits know they have lost you.
    - You quote the Word of God under the anointing and prophesy, and you are hitting the enemy with missiles.
    - The enemy is knocked back and paralyzed.
    - When things clear and the devils leave, all kinds of manifestations and bondages will change because it was all demonic.
    - The first step is establishing your heart in relationships with God and reaffirming your authority.
    - The warfare we go through with the cloudiness and uncertainty of what God is saying and doing in our lives is because we want to know clearly what God wants us to do.

- When I was in Heaven, I saw clearly, and fogginess is caused by evil spirits creating confusion in people.

    - Realize that there will be warfare when we are not doing what God wants us to do.

- You need to be more aggressive in the Spirit against warfare in the environment.
- You need to be in prayer, meditate on the Word of God, and prophesy out loud so that the evil spirits can hear it.
- Then the demons get stirred up, throw a fit, and get pushed back.
- Spend more time alone and shut yourself off for an hour or more.
- Listen to what the Lord is saying and see that it is bright and you are just in a war, but you are going to go through it.

DISCUSSION:

Understand that other people influence you, but be sure you are the one who is dictating. Do not allow other people to bring their war into your arenas. Realize that people will be going through things as well, and you need to be able to manage these things. Unfortunately, you are encountering things that might not be your warfare, but you are called to intercede for them. You must operate accurately by walking in the Spirit and prioritizing your time alone with the Lord in prayer and meditation. Understand that God knows exactly where you are. He loves you, and the Spirit is always willing to cause you to triumph. The Holy Spirit always has the answer, a way, and a route for you to understand and get through anything.

What happens when you are sent?

____

____

____

____

PRAYER

Thank You, Father, that you understand, and are fully convinced, Lord, because you are God. You want to, through Your Spirit, fully convince us and establish us in You. I thank you for Your Spirit, Your Word, and the fact that You have our future. May we be encouraged that You cause us to triumph over our enemies and will cause us to be effective in every way. I break the power of the enemy. I command every spirit of confusion and fear to go in Jesus' name. I break the power of the devil right now over them. I drive out the devils in the name of Jesus. I command you to cease and let go in the name of Jesus. Father, thank You that Your children can see clearly, and You will speak to them and walk them out of whatever it is that they are in. Lord, show them how to triumph in Jesus' name.

CHAPTER 9

Beyond Requesting

For assuredly, I say to you, whoever says to this mountain 'Be removed and be cast into the sea,' and does not doubt in his heart, but believes that those things he says will be done, he will have whatever he says. Therefore I say to you, whatever things you ask when you pray, believe that you receive them, *and you will have them.*

—Mark 11:23-24

DISCUSSION:

We think of prayer as requests; we were taught to make our requests known to God, and God will answer (Philippians 4:6). You were left with the thought if He wants to answer, then He will. Or if He does not want to, He won't. To walk in authority, you must know God's will and enforce what God wants because you know Him. The reality is it goes beyond requesting into a knowing that certain things will happen because God wants them to, and we are supposed to do something about it. Sometimes your atmosphere does not change because God wants you to change it—He has given you the authority.

- Evil spirits are all around you, and they know what should be happening as far as God's will is concerned.
- Evil spirits are preventing God's will from happening because they know they will lose a foothold and ground.
- God chose words to be how He created the world from the beginning and made us in His image.
- We became speaking spirits, so we could speak the will of God and bring forth the mysteries.
- God calls things that are not as though they were (Romans 4:17).
- God speaks things into existence out of nothing.
- We are in His image, so we have authority and dominion over everything.
- Everything was created and formed by words, so this is the reason we speak to our mountains (Mark 11:23).

Why did we become speaking spirits?

____

____

____

____

ENFORCE THE KINGDOM

If you enforce the kingdom, you must know the kingdom's rules and the intent of God's role. If God has already said something, then it is already established. You partner with what has been established, and you come in and correct it if it is not that way to make it established. Authority comes in here because law enforcement is enforcing the already established laws.

❖ **COLOSSIANS 1:16:**

For by Him all things were created that are in heaven and that are on earth, visible and invisible, whether thrones or dominions or principalities or powers. All things were created through Him and for Him.

- If something is already established, you do not have to request compliance.
- You demand it because it is already decreed.
- A king sits on his throne, has authority, and speaks from an established throne.
- The king is over a kingdom, and he is over that dominion.
- A king has a domain and gives a decree from the throne, which is the seat of authority.
- The whole domain, the whole kingdom, is under the rule of what the king says because it has already been established.
- We have the Word, and we must know the Word.
- That Word rules everything that has been spoken into existence.

❖ **MATTHEW 6:10:**

Your kingdom come. Your will be done On earth as *it is* in heaven.

- Jesus is a king, and He says, "If you love Me, then you will obey what I have decreed from my throne (John 14:15)" because that is the seat of authority for the kingdom, and you are a partaker.
- You are in God's kingdom, and you will enforce not just believe but enforce those decrees.
- This is where the requests in prayer turn into a demand; if the king says it, that is the way it will be.
- When the king's decrees are not being done, you, as a subject of the King, His kingdom, and part of His family now have a part.
- Now you demand justice, righteousness, and the decree that was spoken, and you can demand that it is enforced on behalf of you or someone else.
- You have to decree, place a demand, and repeat what has already been spoken.
- Authority is more about enforcing than it is about requesting.

DISCUSSION:

When God's kingdom confronts the devil's kingdom, Jesus said to drive out the devils because they are not complying with the kingdom of God. You drive them out because they are trespassing. You are having trouble because you do not understand displacement, that you must drive out devils. After all, there is a decree that has gone forth already. If God's will is not being done, you should feel righteous

indignation because you know something is wrong. You want things to come into compliance with God's perfect will. His kingdom comes; His will be done on earth as it is in Heaven (Matthew 6:10). Now, it is no longer a request but a demand. The devil is behind everything that is being hindered.

❖ **<u>MARK 11:23:</u>**

For assuredly, I say to you, whoever says to this mountain, 'Be removed and be cast into the sea,' and does not doubt in his heart, but believes that those things he says will be done, he will have whatever he says.

- You should not waste time requesting things already established as God's will. When you stand praying, you demand telling it to go and be uprooted and cast into the sea.
- Whatever it is, you have authority to do something about it.
- If the body of Christ did this, it would rid a lot of evil on earth. You have the authority to decree it and forbid certain things from happening.
- If we agree as touching it, it will be done.
- Your words are powerful in the Spirit, but you must agree with what God has said.
- Mountains can be moved, and Jesus said that we should do this.
- Do not doubt but believe in your heart that what you say with your mouth will come to pass.
- You must be fully convinced that mountains move, and trees are uprooted. You must be fully convinced and trust in God's authority.
- If God has revealed it to you, it is His will and no longer a request.

- There are demanding prayers because the enemy is withholding the provision.
- The enemy withholds God's perfect will and must be addressed aggressively and affirmative.
- God's will is not always done if we do not act.
- If a mountain needs to be addressed, it will stay there until it is addressed.

Why is God's will not done?

____

____

____

____

MISREPRESENTING HIM

DISCUSSION:

Jesus came against doubt and fear because He knew these demonic spirits were coming against people, and they had not been fully convinced. You must have faith and be in full authority because we understand the decree that has been given to us by God on His throne in His kingdom, and we are enforcing it. Then the devils must go. Jesus shows us how to implement the other realm. Now you know you were waiting for God to show you if it was His will or not, and it is not contrary to His Word and His personality, so you know it is the enemy, and you need to stand up against it. In Malachi, we can see that the Lord was upset with them because they were speaking against the Lord and their words were harsh.

- **MALACHI 3:13-14:**

  "Your words have been harsh against Me," Says the Lord, "Yet you say, 'What have we spoken against You?' You have said, 'It is useless to serve God; What profit is it that we have kept His ordinance, And that we have walked as mourners Before the Lord of hosts?

- The people were speaking contrary to the truth about God.
- They were speaking against the Lord, and He was upset with them.
- They were misrepresenting Him.
- Another group of people at the time decided that God was faithful, and it *does* pay to serve God, and they spoke well of the Lord.
- They did not misrepresent the Lord with their words and were not against God.
- If you attribute things that have happened to you as God doing it, and it was not God but the enemy doing it, you will be held accountable for every idle word that comes out of your mouth (Matthew 12:36).
- Do not allow harsh words to come out of your mouth against the Lord.

What will happen if you attribute the enemy's work to the work of God?

____

____

____

____

- **<u>MATTHEW 12:31-32:</u>**

"Therefore I say to you, every sin and blasphemy will be forgiven men, but the blasphemy against the Spirit will not be forgiven men. Anyone who speaks a word against the Son of Man, it will be forgiven him; but whoever speaks against the Holy Spirit, it will not be forgiven him, either in this age or in the age to come.

- When you speak against the Holy Spirit, there is no forgiveness.
- You cannot attribute the works of the devil to the works of God.
- You cannot say that praying in the Spirit is of the devil because the Holy Spirit gives the utterance.
- Our words need to enforce God's goodness, and He is a rewarder of those who diligently seek Him (Hebrews 11:6).
- God is on your side and is working with you.
- The Spirit of God will side with you, and you will be able to speak to mountains.
- You must remember not to let your prayers be hindered because of offense and go and get it right.
- Then you can speak to your mountain, and it will be removed.
- What hinders people is unforgiveness.
- Never make the mistake of saying that bad things came from God.

❖ **<u>JOHN 10:10:</u>**

The thief does not come except to steal, and to kill, and to destroy. I have come that they may have life, and that they may have *it* more abundantly.

- It is the enemy who comes to steal, kill and destroy.
- Jesus has come to give you life and life more abundantly.
- If you have identified the thief, you demand it to be driven out and pay back whatever was stolen—sevenfold. That is the way it is with God's justice system. Start removing mountains in your life.
- The devils do not want you to be effective and discern what God wants to give you. So, you can put a demand and use your authority to take back what has already been decreed.
- You can speak to your body and command it to be healed. You can command your finances to come in line.
- I do not even pray or request finances because I speak to my finances and speak to the enemy and command him to let go of any finances.
- As you pray in tongues, the Spirit will take hold of the will of God, which is beyond what we can operate in.
- As we yield, there is a demand in the area of authority in prayer, and His Spirit will take us further.
- The Spirit will want to take you to a place where mountains start to move, trees get uprooted, and things in your life will be removed.

❖ PHILIPPIANS 3:12-14

Not that I have already attained, or am already perfected; but I press on, that I may lay hold of that for which Christ Jesus has also laid hold of me. Brethren, I do not count myself to have apprehended; but one thing *I do,* forgetting those things which are behind and reaching forward to those things which are ahead, I press toward the goal for the prize of the upward call of God in Christ Jesus.

- The Spirit will take hold of that which Christ has already taken hold of for you.
- You will obtain the promises, and you have been given everything needed for life and godliness, and it is already inside you.
- So, yield to that; you do not need to request anymore. Just believe God right now, and you are going to resolve that.
- There are certain things you do not need to be fasting about anymore.
- You do not even need to be requesting anymore.
- You need to put your foot down in the Spirit, speak it out of your mouth, and command these things to move and get out of your way.
- You can speak the perfect will of God and say that God wants to heal you because Jesus already paid for it.
- Jesus gives you everything you need for life and godliness (2 Peter 1:3).
- He supplies your needs above what you could ask or think according to His riches and glory. God already said that!
- You do not have to request—you can demand it now because God has already spoken.

What happens when you pray in the Spirit?

____

____

____

____

PRAYER

Lord, we thank You for supplying all of our needs according to Your riches and glory. Release boldness in the name of Jesus. Thank You that all the power and boldness in the Spirit is coming upon your people, and they can address and speak from the Spirit knowing that those mountains will move. Thank You that we are no longer requesting but demanding in the name of Jesus.

CHAPTER 10

Beyond Logic

And Enoch walked with God; and he was not, for God took him.

—Genesis 5:24

DISCUSSION:

Another aspect of relationship with God is authority, and not just in our position in Christ. We see this in God's relationship with Abraham, Moses, King David, and Enoch. We can glean from the fact that Enoch pleased God so much that God took him. Enoch would have been more effective in remaining on the earth and walking with that relationship because he could affect many people, but God was so pleased that He just wanted Enoch for Himself. When you think about this, it goes beyond any kind of logic. If the Lord had chosen for me to stay in Heaven, then none of Warrior Notes would have been established, affecting people worldwide. Enoch pleased God so much that God took him, and Enoch forfeited any influence he would have had on the earth. Enoch walked in a relationship with God, and God made that decision. A part of kingdom authority has to do with relationship. Some people will remain hidden and not be made public because God wants them for Himself. No

matter what God says in His Word, He has feelings and passion. God took to certain individuals, they had favor, and things happened that went beyond logic. Certain individuals could talk to God on a higher level, such as Moses talking to God face to face.

- ❖ I know something about God: if you sit and talk to Him, you are in agreement because He has already established and planned, and there will be no resistance. I experienced this when I was in Heaven, so we got along because I decided not to have my way, so I handed over my will.

    - I started to see things happen that were beyond what I could ever do on my own or even believe for.
    - Much of it is favor because I turn myself over to Him in my will and agree with Him.
    - Things will bypass your understanding, and you will not process things by deciding for yourself because you have turned over your will.
    - When you have this kind of relationship, you are given authority.

Why did God take Enoch?

____

____

____

____

BEYOND RELATIONSHIP

I noticed that certain things are not spoken, and God does them because He knows your heart and does things you never asked for because of relationship. He does something, and it has nothing to do with your faith, and it doesn't have to do with you asking or receiving. He has said to me whatever you want, decide what you want, and I will do it.

❖ **<u>EPHESIANS 3:20:</u>**

Now to Him who is able to do exceedingly abundantly above all that we ask or think, according to the power that works in us.

- I noticed that certain things are not spoken, and God does them because He knows your heart and does things you never asked for because of relationship.
- God does something, and it has nothing to do with your faith, and it does not have to do with you asking or receiving.
- The Lord once said, "Whatever you want, decide what you want, and I will do it."
- When He does what you want, it is because of relationship and trust.
- It has nothing to do with having faith and convincing ourselves of something or seeking God and trying to find His will in a certain manner.
- Sometimes, God will say, "I am doing this for you even if you did not ask for it, or "You just decide what you want, and I will do it."

Why does God do what you want?

____

____

____

____

DISCIPLINED PATH

DISCUSSION:

After being saved for five or six years, I walked into a disciplined path, and it was a narrow path. I was not allowed to do what everyone else was allowed to do. I had a vision, and the Lord was telling me to do this and not that; it was a very disciplined life. I could hear the Spirit of God very clearly, but it was hard and required a lot of fasting, praying, and being alone, and it was not what I wanted to do. The vision was an open field but a narrow path in the woods, which was very constrictive. There was only one way to go through it. I experienced this for six years, and then it started to end. Then I saw a vision of an open field, and it came to an opening, and the path led to a field with beautiful flowers and birds, and it was bright and sunny. Finally, the Lord said He was giving me freedom because I submitted to the yoke of learning.

❖ **HEBREWS 12:5-7 NLT:**

And have you forgotten the encouraging words God spoke to you as his children? He said, "My child, don't make light of the LORD's discipline, and don't give up when he corrects you. For the LORD disciplines those he loves, and he punished each one he accepts as his child." As you endure this divine

discipline, remember that God is treating you as his own children. Who ever heard of a child who is never disciplined by its father?

- My years of being disciplined by the Lord now caused me to be trusted by Him.
- Now when I asked for things, He would say, "Whatever you want, you can do it. What do you want to do?"
- Now I concentrate on what is in my heart, and it is an open field through a relationship developed through discipline.
- I have matured and can be trusted to make the right decisions and yield to the Spirit in everything.

According to Hebrews 12:5-7, what does the Lord do to those He loves?

____

____

____

____

❖ I believe this is going to happen to you also. You have submitted to the teachings of the Bible and the Spirit of God and are learning to walk with Him. You will be disciplined enough that He is going to trust you. In that trust, you will be able to make mature decisions. He is going to tell you that you can do whatever you desire.

- You have learned how to listen to your heart, and you will not choose the wrong things.
- The Lord wants you to operate in authority in any situation you find yourself in.
- Start to implement and help people to establish their walk with God.
- As leaders, walk in this and discern those you disciple and talk to them, speak to them and invest in them.
- Find out what is in your heart and do it. It could be feeding the poor, helping single moms, helping kids, etc.

How can the Lord trust you?

____

____

____

____

ONE WITH HIM

❖ **JOHN 10:30:**

I and *My* Father are one.

- I remember the Spirit being grieved if I would say something contrary to what the Lord was saying.
- All of this changed after I was disciplined and learned the ways of the Spirit, and I learned not to talk at certain times.

- You will say, "Lord, I want You to show me and tell me what You want."
- Then you get to the place where the Lord says, what do you want?
- You have matured, and you will know, listen and do exactly what He wants.
- You have finally matured, and you are one with Him.
- The limits are going to come off because the Lord trusts you.
- God is not purposely holding anything back from you.
- God's will is revealed to you, and He will show you your future.
- God will help you; He trusts you, and the limitations will be removed.
- No one in Heaven is holding you back. Everyone in Heaven agrees with you, including the Trinity and the angels.
- Certain things are written about you that must come to pass and be accomplished.
- In every generation, certain things are already established for people to do.

DISCUSSION:

You can never exhaust everything you are supposed to do because so much has defaulted because people are not doing it—for instance, playing instruments. After all, other people didn't do it. I have had to pick things up and do what others were supposed to do. Why? Because the body of Christ still needs these things done. So many more revelations, songs, books, and study guides must come forth—it is endless. It could go on forever because you can never exhaust everything. After all, there will always be something that the Spirit will want to bring forth.

- ❖ I will speak from the Spirit, helping people, nudging them toward good works, so the limits are off. Things now default to those who have been faithful with what they have been given.

    - The books in Heaven (Psalm 139:16) represent this because God, in His foreknowledge, knew.
    - You need to insert yourself into the perfect will of God and be connected, praying in the Holy Spirit because things will evolve.
    - Everything will increase, and there will be no end—there is no real limit.
    - You will be surprised at what was added to you and your life and what God has for you.
    - Everything is rigged in your favor because of the blood of Jesus. The blood can never be limited because it takes care of everything.
    - Jesus' blood was enough to wipe away everyone's sin.
    - We do not know the value of what God has planned that is in you already, but the Holy Spirit does.
    - You need to yield to a limitless God who does not have any limits on you; it is through relationship.
    - Pray this, "Lord, make me willing to be willing."
    - Give Him permission to change your heart and change the way you feel or think. Pray and build yourself up.
    - Then pray, "Lord, break my will. Cause me to be able to go further with You and not limit myself based on what I know. Take me further than I know by showing me."

How do you get to the place where the Lord says, what do you want?

____

____

____

____

THE HOLY SPIRIT IS YOUR FRIEND

❖ **JOHN 14:26 MSG:**

The Friend, the Holy Spirit whom the Father will send at my request, will make everything plain to you. He will remind you of all the things I have told you.

- The Spirit of God became my friend.

❖ **HEBREWS 4:12:**

For the word of God *is* living and powerful, and sharper than any two-edged sword, piercing even to the division of soul and spirit, and of joints and marrow, and is a discerner of the thoughts and intents of the heart.

- The Word of God is a sword. The sword is the Spirit of God and the Word, and it divides between the soul and the spirit.

- When He comes in, you need to pray, "Lord, make me willing to be willing." Then God's Word, His Spirit, divides between your soul (your mind, will, and emotions) and your spirit, which is the real you.
- The Spirit and the Word divide between the things God has already established for you and your psychological makeup.
- You have a mind, a will, and emotions that are your soul, but your spirit is born again.
- The Word of God, the Spirit of God, comes in like a sword, and cuts, divides, separates, and clarifies what your soul or the Spirit is.
- God reveals things to you in your life, such as *this is you, and this is what you want*, but *this is what God wants.*
- It is already in you, and it is the Spirit, and it is the Word that causes it to become separate.
- People need not waste time but invest in their spiritual life by concentrating on praying in the Spirit, knowing what the Spirit wants, and meditating on God's will, which is His Word.
- The Word and the Spirit form a two-edged sword, and then you can be sharp and divide between what is in you and God's will for your life.
- God knows you, and you are known in Heaven because you speak to Him, honor Him, and He honors you, and He asks you, "What do you want?"
- This is where the church is going. When Jesus comes back for the church, this is the condition of the church.

What does the two-edged sword of the Word of God and the Spirit do?

____

____

____

____

❖ **<u>1 JOHN 3:2:</u>**

Beloved, now we are children of God; and it has not yet been revealed what we shall be, but we know that when He is revealed, we shall be like Him, for we shall see Him as He is.

- The sons of God will be revealed on earth, and we will see Him as He is, and we will be like Him, but we will address Him as a fellow heir.
- Jesus is a fellow heir. We are heirs of God and co-heirs with Jesus Christ (Romans 8:17).

Do you have a friend relationship with the Holy Spirit?

____

____

____

____

DISCUSSION:

According to John 17, we share in God's glory, love, and unity. Jesus addressed those three things, and as believers, we are sharing in that now through Him. We have a relationship. We can talk to God without limitations. We can rightly divide what is inside us by the Spirit and by the Word and know the perfect will of God. I know when something is not right and when it is right. I know when things are supposed to go a certain way, and they do not happen because I know what God wants. We all need to be able to do this, and we will help ourselves and help others. We all need to get into unity and maturity, and then Jesus will come back for His bride.

PRAYER

Father, I thank You for the power of the Holy Spirit and that everyone will feel loved and valued. Bring them into this maturity where we see that open field, that beautiful open field, and you can say to us, "I trust you. What do you want?" We will respond, in relationship and authority, knowing that we are partners, partakers of the divine nature, and can be trusted. Lord, we can make decisions for Your kingdom because You have trained us. We can use the authority given to us with wisdom. Thank You, Lord, that all the limitations are off in the name of Jesus, Amen

SALVATION PRAYER

Lord God,

I confess that I am a sinner.

I confess that I need Your Son, Jesus.

Please forgive me in His name.

Lord Jesus, I believe You died for me and that You

are alive and listening to me now.

I now turn from my sins and welcome

You into my heart. Come and take control of my life.

Make me the kind of person You want me to be.

Now, fill me with Your Holy Spirit, who will show me how to live for You.

I acknowledge You before men as my Savior and my Lord.

In Jesus' name. Amen.

If you prayed this prayer, please contact us at **info@kevinzadai.com** for more information and material.

We welcome you to join our network at Warriornotes.tv for access to exclusive programming

To enroll in our ministry school, go to: Warriornotesschool.com

Visit KevinZadai.com for additional ministry materials

About Dr. Kevin Zadai

Kevin Zadai, Th.D., was called to the ministry at the age of ten. He attended Central Bible College in Springfield, Missouri, where he received a Bachelor of Arts in theology. Later, he received training in missions at Rhema Bible College and a Th. D. at Primus University. Dr. Kevin L. Zadai is dedicated to training Christians to live and operate in two realms at once— the supernatural and the natural. At age 31, Kevin met Jesus, got a second chance at life, and received a revelation that he could not fail because it's all rigged in our favor! Kevin holds a commercial pilot license and is retired from Southwest Airlines after twenty-nine years as a flight attendant. Kevin is the founder and president of Warrior Notes School of Ministry. He and his lovely wife, Kathi, reside in New Orleans, Louisiana.

Other Books and Study Guides By Dr. Kevin Zadai

Kevin has written over fifty books and study guides

Please see our website for a complete list of materials!

Kevinzadai.com

60-Day Healing Devotional

60-Day Devotional: Encountering the Heavenly Sapphire

60-Day Devotional: The Holy Spirit

60-Day Devotional: Supernatural Finances

The Agenda of Angels

The Agenda of Angels: Study Guide

A Meeting Place with God, The Heavenly Encounters Series Volume 1

Days of Heaven on Earth

Days of Heaven on Earth: A Study Guide to the Days Ahead

Days of Heaven on Earth: Prayer and Confession Guide

Encountering God's Normal

Encountering God's Normal: Study Guide

Encountering God's Will

Encountering the Heavenly Sapphire: Study Guide

From Breakthrough to Overthrow: Study Guide

Have you Been to the Altar Lately?

Heavenly Visitation

Heavenly Visitation: Study Guide

Heavenly Visitation: Prayer and Confession Guide

How to Minister to the Sick: Study Guide

It's Rigged in Your Favor

It's all Rigged in Your Favor: Study Guide

It's Time to Take Back Our Country

Lord Help Me to Understand Myself: Study Guide

Mystery of the Power Words

Mystery of the Power Words: Study Guide

The Notes of a Warrior: The Secrets of Spiritual Warfare Volume 1: Study Guide

The Notes of a Warrior: The Secrets of Spiritual Warfare Volume 2: Study Guide

The Power of Creative Worship: Study Guide

Prayer Nations With Kevin & Kathi Zadai

Praying from the Heavenly Realms

Praying from the Heavenly Realms: Study Guide

Precious Blood of Jesus: Study Guide

Receiving from Heaven

Receiving from Heaven: Study Guide

Spiritual Discernment: Study Guide

Stories from the Glory with Sister Ruth Carneal

Supernatural Finances

Supernatural Finances: Study Guide

Supernatural Prayer Strategies of a Warrior: Study Guide

Taking a Stand Against the Enemy

Taking Off the Limitations

Taking Off the Limitations: Study Guide

The Vision and Battle Strategies of Warrior Notes Intl.

Unveiling the Mystery of the Prophetic: Study Guide

Warrior Fellowships Season 1 Volume 1: Study Guide

Warrior Fellowships Season 1 Volume 2: Study Guide

Warrior Notes Aviation Volume 1: Flight Manual Study Guide

Warrior Women Volume 1: Study Guide

Warrior Women Volume 2: Study Guide

Warrior Justice: A Study Guide to Experiencing Freedom from Demonic Oppression

You Can Hear God's Voice

You Can Hear God's Voice: Study Guide